DATE DUE

THE TWELVE DAYS
24 July to 4 August 1914

On July 24, 1914—twenty-six days after the assassination of the Archduke Franz Ferdinand—the Austrian government delivered its long delayed ultimatum to the Serbs. From that day to the British declaration of war on August 4, the decisions were taken, the blunders were made, and in the end there was no escaping the war that changed the course of history.

In this dramatic account of the twelve days preceding the outbreak of war, George Malcolm Thomson brilliantly shows how a tangle of apparently unrelated strands—political and diplomatic maneuvers, private frustrations and ambitions, quirks of personality among Europe's leading figures, ironies of circumstance—combined to produce completely unsought consequences.

After a sharply drawn profile of pre-war Europe, he presents a graphic day-by-day picture of the drama as it unfolded throughout the Continent. There are depictions of vast mobilizations and bursts of patriotic fervor; of quickly stifled pacifist protests; of frivolous celebrations and poignant farewells. There are illuminating word-portraits of Kaiser Wilhelm,

ar, diplomats and generals, and :ss lesser figures who played a · were caught up in the tragedy. ; the more notable personalities urès, the French Socialist leadose assassination by a fanatic anti-war sentiments in France; Caillaux, wife of the French er of Finance, fighting for her ι sensational murder trial which ister political overtones; Count old, the Austrian Foreign Min-ι trifler leading his country to r; and Sir Edward Grey, the hman who sought peace and ιt war.

:se are only a few of the actors ιppear upon the scene, which from Paris to the Baltic, from tersburg to Vienna, from Lon-ι a remote Balkan railway junc-Skillfully weaving a mass of detail into a gripping, swiftly paced account of the Old World hovering on the brink of destruction, Mr. Thomson has produced an unforgettable evocation of the last days of peace in Europe's fatal summer.

GEORGE MALCOLM THOMSON

The Twelve Days
24 July to 4 August 1914

7494

G. P. PUTNAM'S SONS
NEW YORK

To
LORD BEAVERBROOK,
witness
and matchless historian
of those days,
in admiration and affection.

D 511
.T47
1964

Acknowledgements

I owe a special debt to Luigi Albertini's *The Origins of the War of
1914*, an intricate and masterly unravelling of the diplomatic
evidence. Albertini is an indispensable authority for this time
and, at many points, I have been content to follow his guidance.
I am grateful to the Oxford University Press for permission to
use the material in this way.

I must thank Victor Gollancz Ltd. for the permission they
generously gave me to quote from Theodor Wolff's admirable
first-hand impressions in *The Eve of 1914*. Sir Edward Spears and
William Heinemann Ltd. have put me in their debt by allowing
me to quote from *Liaison 1914* extracts which vividly convey
the atmosphere of Paris. Martin Secker and Warburg Ltd. have
kindly allowed me to use first-hand material quoted in Richard
Thoumin's *The Great War* which they publish in Britain. I am
grateful for this courtesy. I must also thank J. M. Dent and Sons
Ltd., publishers of Joseph Conrad's *Notes on Life and Letters*, for
allowing me to quote from this book. Macmillan and Co. Ltd.
have given me permission to quote from Lord Morley's *Memorandum on Resignation* extracts which throw light on the internal
struggle in the Asquith Cabinet. From Sir Harold Nicolson I
have had a characteristically generous permission to quote from
his biographies, *King George the Fifth* and *Sir Arthur Nicolson
Bart., First Lord Carnock*. Both works are published by Constable.
I am grateful to the author and the publishers. John Murray
(Publishers) Ltd. kindly allow me to make extracts from Cecily
Mackworth's *Guillaume Apollinaire* which they publish. For brief,
but valuable, excerpts from Stefan Zweig's *The World of Yesterday* I owe my thanks to Cassell and Co. Ltd. I must also express
my debt to Leon Trotsky's *My Life* for incomparable glimpses
of Vienna in 1914.

ACKNOWLEDGEMENTS

I have to thank Lord Rosebery for permission to quote from a letter giving his personal recollections of Longchamps, 28 June 1914; Sir Norman Angell for his help in tracing the history of the Neutrality League; Mr. Gerard Fay who courteously made it possible for me to see the 1914 files of the *Manchester Guardian*; Mr. Willi Frischauer, who helped me with the Captain of Koepenick; Mr. C. M. Houghton for his account of the cancelled Esperanto Congress; Mr. Hugo Garten and Mrs. M. Dernbach for assistance with works in German.

Mr. A. J. P. Taylor kindly read the book in typescript and made valuable suggestions which I gratefully acknowledge.

I have received advice (not always taken) and help from Mr. John Raymond, Mr. Ronald Spark, Mr. James McMillan and Miss Judy Sheehan. I am deeply obliged to them.

The copyright in the photograph of Count Berchtold (opposite p. 65) belongs to Paul Popper Ltd.; the End of the Race (opposite p. 64) and the two illustrations of the Caillaux Trial (opposite p. 80) belong to Les Éditions de l'Illustration; and 'The Neutrality League' (opposite p. 161) is the property of *The Guardian*; all other photographs come from Radio Times Hulton Picture Library.

G. M. T.

Contents

3
AFTERMATH

Illustrations will be found
following page 100.

I

PRELUDE

Each national flag in turn has had its gleam of glory: often enough, by some turn of fortune, great victories have been followed by great defeats. Today a finer arena offers itself to the sovereigns of Europe.

NAPOLEON, April 1815

One knows where a war begins but one never knows where it ends.

BERNHARD VON BÜLOW, 1898

'Jamais le ciel plus beau, ni le bonheur
plus mûr, La vie plus désirable.'
                    PAUL VALÉRY

1

Sunday at the Races

THERE was not a cloud in the sky.
Somewhere beyond the flower-beds, as garish as gypsies, beyond the lawns and the ample trees, the bewitching city shimmered in the heat. Longchamps, at the peak of the Grande Semaine. Sunday afternoon, 28 June 1914.

The President and his wife had driven through the Bois in state. The band had played. Grey top-hats had been raised, white-gloved hands had come to the brim of képis. And there he sat in the Presidential box, his features too grey, too compressed, for so frivolous an occasion. Into this light-hearted gathering there had wandered, as it seemed, some tight-fisted provincial notary.

Strolling round the paddock, men admired the horses and judged the women. Women admired the horses and looked at

15

one another. With more interest, they studied the clothes their sisters were wearing.

The dictator Paul Poiret had decreed 'Let the bust be liberated and the legs be fettered!' His subjects had hastened to obey, each according to her taste and status. In black and white, in muslin, with pearls and wide-brimmed hats, they appeared: the women of society, the mannequins and those other women who, to the letter of the edict, added their own nuance of provocation. Here and there, in the crowd, and indeed scattered through the Bois and in church porches and other likely places in the city, were vendors of 'the little blue flower', sold that day for the Red Cross Society.

Very soon a respectful hush would fall. At a few minutes after four the most valuable race of the year would be run. The Grand Prix de Paris with £16,000 of prize-money to be won, and not an English horse thought worthy to compete. In so gay a setting Lords Granard, Sefton, Dalmeny and Castlereagh forgot any patriotic chagrin they might feel.[1]

It was thought that Baron Maurice de Rothschild's Sardanapale would win, although Baron Edmond de Rothschild's Farina had its followers.

So idle, so busy was the crowd that very few noticed the officer of the President's entourage who, just before four o'clock when the starter was about to give the signal to the jockeys, handed M. Poincaré a telegram from the Havas Agency. The President read it and, without any change of expression, passed it to Count Szecsen, the Austro-Hungarian ambassador, a spry, elderly Magyar, who sat nearby. Szecsen read the message. It contained the news that the Archduke Franz Ferdinand of

---

1. Lord Rosebery (in 1914, Lord Dalmeny) writes: 'It was a boiling hot day and a wonderful race. We had an English party with whom was Count Charles Kinsky. He was an Austrian, but more English than the English. He had ridden the winner of the Grand National, Zoedone. When the news of the assassination of the Archduke Franz Ferdinand was made known on the racecourse, most of us did not realize that war was inevitable, but he did. He left the course immediately and I never saw him again.'

Habsburg-Este, heir apparent to the Austro-Hungarian throne, had been murdered along with his morganatic wife, the Duchess of Hohenberg, while on a state visit to Sarajevo in Bosnia. Bosnians, it seemed, had done the deed.

Excusing himself to the President, Szecsen rose and hurried from the course.

The Balkan town which a tragic event snatched from obscurity stands at the mouth of a river-gorge. The white walls and red roofs of Old Sarajevo are picturesquely scattered over wooded hillsides. Above its houses rise minarets and domes; in Sarajevo 50,000 people are divided equally between the Moslem or Jewish faiths and the Christian, Orthodox or Catholic. In the centre of the town is the bazaar, a labyrinth of fifty narrow lanes crowded with booths. Here the Moslem craftsmen are dominant.

The Archduke Franz Ferdinand was making a military visit to Bosnia in his capacity as commander-in-chief of the Austrian army. He and his wife drove into the town in the second of four motor-cars. Opposite them sat the Governor of Bosnia, Oskar Potiorek. In front with the driver was Count Harrach, head of the motor corps. As they came near the city hall the crowds were dense and the popular welcome was gratifying if not enthusiastic. At half past ten something struck the hood of the car behind the royal pair. It fell into the road, and exploded when the third car passed. Two officers of the Archduke's suite were wounded, one of them seriously. The Archduke ordered his car to stop. Meanwhile, the man who had thrown the bomb fled over the bridge that spans the river at that point. He was caught by the police. He turned out to be a young compositor named Cabrinovitch.

'So you welcome your guests with bombs!' exclaimed the Archduke furiously. As best he could, the burgomaster made his speech of welcome. The imperial and royal guest recovered his composure sufficiently to reply, reading in his thin, high-pitched voice from a manuscript spattered with his aide-de-camp's blood. Then he announced that he would go alone to the hospital to visit the wounded officer. His wife, however, insisted on going with him: if there was danger that was only the better reason why she should be at his side.

When Count Harrach said he was astonished to discover that there was no military guard to protect the heir to the throne, Potiorek sneered, 'Do you think Sarajevo is full of assassins?' There were only 120 policemen in the town and no soldiers, although two Austrian army corps were in the neighbourhood.

The four cars drove off once more, faster than before and along a route different from that which had been announced. Count Harrach stood on the running-board of the Archduke's car, a drawn sword in his hand. There were few police about. By a mistake, the first car turned into Franz Josef Strasse, which had been on the original route. The Archduke's driver was about to follow when Potiorek corrected him, so that the car went forward at a slow pace along the riverside quay. Two shots were fired from a distance of less than ten feet.

Sarajevo was full of assassins.

Potiorek excitedly ordered the driver to find another bridge over the river. Only then did he realize that blood was gushing from the Archduke's mouth over his green uniform. His wife was leaning on him, unconscious but with no visible wound. 'Sophie, Sophie, live for our children,' gasped the Archduke. They were carried to a room in the Koniak (the government building) next to one in which the champagne was cooling for lunch. A quarter of an hour later both were dead.

The murderer was seized by the crowd. He had taken cyanide but his body had rejected it. He was a Serb student, an Austrian subject, named Gabriel Princip.

About the same time as the interruption at Longchamps, 500 miles to the north-east, in Kiel Bay, all pearly light in the Baltic afternoon, Admiral von Müller in the steam launch *Hulda* was hurrying after the imperial yacht *Meteor* racing on a northerly course towards the Danish islands. The Kaiser himself was at the helm. When Müller waved a signal to heave-to, Wilhelm answered with an impatient wave. The Admiral shouted into the wind, 'I bring grave news.' He put a decoded telegram from the German Consul-General at Sarajevo into his cigarette case and prepared to throw it aboard the yacht. But the Kaiser insisted on hearing the news by word of mouth. It is reported that he said, 'Everything has to be started over again.' He ordered that the race should be abandoned. An Austrian guest on the *Meteor* was in his cabin, seasick. On hearing the news, he recovered at once.

In the imperial villa at Bad Ischl the Emperor Franz Joseph of Austria reconciled himself to the tidings from Sarajevo with the alacrity of one who, being very old, was accustomed to the idea of death. 'Frightful, frightful,' he said, and then, with more animation: 'The Almighty is not defied with impunity. The order which I was, alas, unable to maintain, a Higher Will has re-established.' He was thinking of the Archduke's marriage to the Bohemian Countess Sophie Chotek. The aged dynast was apt to confuse the secret law of the House of Habsburg with the ordinances of heaven.

Baden is a pleasant little spa in the hills of Vienna, smelling slightly of sulphur. The Biedermeir houses have kept some charm from the days when Beethoven used to stay there in summer. And this June the woods were exceptionally rich and beautiful. The town was full of visitors from Vienna who had arrived, as usual, for the feast of SS. Peter and Paul next day. One of these, a young man of thirty-three, named Stefan Zweig, sat in the Kurpark, reading a book and listening to the band. When the music stopped suddenly he looked up. The crowd seemed no longer to be strolling idly about. The bandsmen had left the stand. People were crowding round, peering excitedly at a notice which had been posted up. Zweig went forward and read it. He remembered the Archduke whom he had often seen in the theatre. 'There he sat in his box, broad and mighty, with cold, fixed gaze, never casting a single friendly glance towards the audience or encouraging the actors with hearty applause. . . . His wife was equally unfriendly.'

Alexander Musulin, head of Chancery at the Austrian Foreign Office, was among the visitors in Baden that day. He heard the news in the garden of the Zum Grünen Baum Hotel there and set off at once for the Ballhausplatz.

At Longchamps the yellow-and-green was first past the post: after a great race Baron Maurice's Sardanapale won by a neck. Lucky gamblers collected eighteen francs on a stake of five.

Prince von Bülow, former German Chancellor, was sitting solicitously at the bedside of his friend Frau von Lebbin in Berlin when the telephone rang. It was Paul von Schwabach, the banker, who had just learned of the tragedy in Sarajevo.

The Prince bore the tidings with the sang-froid of one who has expected no good news since he had ceased to guide his country's policy. Later he condoled with Count Szogyenyi, the Austrian ambassador. The Count, with a pious glance at the ceiling, replied that, while as a Christian and a Hungarian nobleman he deplored the Archduke's fate, politically speaking the elimination of the heir to the throne was a blessing of Providence. *Requiescat in pace.*

The Archduke had once said, 'It was bad taste of the Magyars ever to come to Europe.'

The news was recived with even greater resignation in Rome. For some time the Italian government had been trying to buy the Villa d'Este at Tivoli from the Archduke, its owner. The Foreign Minister, San Giuliano, rang up the Prime Minister: 'Is that you, Salandra? We shall have no more bother about the Villa d'Este affair. This morning they've murdered the Archduke.'

President Poincaré, bowling back to the Elysée at a good pace, was preoccupied with graver—but stimulating—thoughts. It was more important than ever that he should make his state visit to St. Petersburg: that he should see the Tsar, and put a little steel into the backbone of that mighty, doubtful ally.

When Musulin arrived in Vienna the city was made sinister in the sunlight by the black flags which draped its buildings.

The Belvedere Palace, built for Prince Eugene of Savoy and, until a few hours earlier, the residence of the Archduke, looked forlornly down over its clipped yew hedges at the spires and the domes of the city and the vast bulk of St. Stephen's shouldering itself out of the mass of buildings. The Belvedere was the finest of the imperial palaces, and its baroque roofs, like tents of the Tartars turned into copper, reminded a spectator that it had been created as the palace of a famous soldier.

In the Kärntner Strasse groups of people studied extra editions of the newspapers. Everywhere Musulin heard the same remark: 'We can't put up with any more of this. This time it's war.'

Another man who witnessed the excitement in the streets was Musulin's chief, Count Berchtold, the Austrian Foreign Minister. He had been opening a charity bazaar at his country seat in Moravia when the news of the assassination of his friend the Archduke reached him. He had caught the next train to Vienna. Berchtold knew that the Austrian empire faced a supreme crisis. He saw it in simple terms: either Serbia would be brought under control or the empire would disintegrate. During the weeks that followed, he sought the first objective. But destiny, helped by Poincaré's implacable nature and by desperate counsels in St. Petersburg, had her own more terrible design.

2

Portrait of a Prospective Suicide

THE Europe through which one brutal event resounded so ominously was already filled with an accumulation of wealth, power, culture and menace. Into it, in ancient times, the tribes had flocked from Asia and had paused for a millennium, as if gathering strength for the leap which would carry them to the farther shores of the ocean. In the meantime they had grown edges and histories, and loyalties subtler and more implacable than those of the clan.

Six great cultures—and as many lesser ones—had come to life on the soil of the Continent and had thrust their roots deeply between its rocks. By turns tending and neglecting their garden, its peoples had built and burnt a score of civilizations, gathered wealth with avarice and squandered it in bursts of princely recklessness. The final harvest was an economic ascendancy greater than any that had ever been known.

Half of the coal burnt in the world was dug out of Europe's mines; 60 per cent of the world's steel came from European furnaces and three out of every four merchant ships flew European flags. At the same time it had strewn its resources across the globe with a prodigal hand.

In the hundred years since Waterloo it had sent overseas 40,000,000 of its sons and daughters.[1] With the people had gone the money. Britain alone, pampered offshore island of a favoured continent, had invested £4000,000,000 in America or elsewhere. France, the other chief banker of the globe, owned more than £1000,000,000 of foreign investments, although this money was not so wisely placed as Britain's. One-third of the French loans were in Russia on a military mission.[1]

One might have supposed, contemplating so extravagant an effusion of wealth, that this continent was unable to employ at home any more of its capital. But this would not have been exact.

The children of Europe ruled half of Asia and almost all of Africa. The states of America had been created by their genius, spoke their languages and had rebelled against their domination. In all, Europe was the lord of 225,000,000 colonial subjects. And, in addition, there was India, an Asiatic empire administered by a few hundred English and Scots. Since the days of Roman rule there had been nothing like the world suzerainty of Europe.

All this wealth and pre-eminence the people of the old continent took for granted, as if unaware that so extraordinary an ascendancy could only, in the nature of things, be of brief duration.

Yet already one could see that dangers to its unique position were coming into being. Great powers were rising outside its bounds to challenge it. And, within, the perils were greater still. Europe had too many frontiers, too many—and too well-remembered—histories, too many soldiers for safety. Five of its states alone kept, in time of peace, armies totalling 3,800,000 soldiers. With so many men dedicated to defence, who could help feeling nervous!

1. And 7,000,000 had emigrated from European to Asiatic Russia.

The populations might have viewed their situation in the world with thankfulness and humility. But the cranky continent, with its miraculous endowment, its wonderful inherited talent, had a notable shortage of good feeling. The spoilt darlings of fortune brooded with envy over a neighbour's wealth or with uneasiness over his strength. No nation in Europe was a friend of any other. At best they might be allies, who had decided to mitigate their mutual distrust or postpone the settlement of their quarrel. It was the smallest, richest and most illustrious of the continents, but how many of its 447,000,000 people took pride in calling themselves Europeans? Each year, too, it grew smaller.

Already an aeroplane could remain in the air for thirteen hours at a stretch and attain a speed of 100 miles an hour. Chavez had flown the Alps, Roland Garros the Mediterranean. While President Poincaré was driving along the Allée des Acacias, on his way back to the Elysée Palace on that Sunday afternoon in June, a Norwegian lieutenant, Trygve Gran, was preparing to fly from Cruden Bay in Scotland to Stavanger in his own country. This he duly accomplished a month later.

Yet still, in this shrinking Europe, 3000 miles across and 2000 miles from north to south, strategists dreamed of conquests and nursed revenges; they dwelt in a wider and emptier Europe which no longer existed. Hopelessly obsolete in speech as well as thought, they still drew flashing swords, still stood in shining armour; and spent millions of money every year in maintaining troops of knights, who, accoutred with cuirass, helmet, lance and sabre, would gallop into battle against—— Against whom? It was as relevant to ask against what?

The machine-gun was already thirty years old. The tank was about to be born. A truck mounted on an endless chain had appeared at the Aldershot review five years before.

If war came to Europe again it would be of a kind and on a scale that had never been seen before. But why, it might be asked, must the possibility of war be reckoned with at all?

Had the question been addressed to any of those who took or influenced the important decisions of state they would have answered simply that war was inevitable. In this respect, Moltke, the German Chief of Staff, a man who had no stomach for a fight, was in complete agreement with Conrad von Hötzendorff, the Austrian Commander-in-Chief, a fire-eater and a hero in the smartest drawing-rooms of Vienna.

What the soldiers believed was echoed by quite intelligent politicians. For example, Comte Albert de Mun wrote in the *Echo de Paris* in 1913: 'All Europe, uncertain and troubled, prepares for an inevitable war, the immediate cause of which remains still unknown to her.'

Under the smooth and smiling surface of the old civilization novel forces were at work and strange collisions of culture were creating a suppressed effervescence. Rarely in all its history had Europe been in such an intellectual ferment.

In 1913 Albert Einstein had published a paper in Zürich which took the first cautious steps towards the general theory of relativity. Almost simultaneously, in Vienna, Sigmund Freud had given his five closest disciples an antique Greek intaglio mounted on a gold ring. The Old Guard of psycho-analysis was mustered. Already Bergson had insisted on the power of the irrational in human behaviour and Nietzsche had proclaimed the part played by force in social transformation. In 1908 Georges Sorel had carried the teachings of these prophets into the realm of politics in a book with the explosive title *Reflections on Violence*.

Thus in physics, psychology, morals and political thinking the old, reasonable, comfortable assumptions of the nineteenth century were challenged and a new age, intoxicated by the intuitive and the brutal, was coming into existence.

The public were ready to experience and simultaneously to resent what was novel and what was foreign. The Russian Ballet excited the West. Paris saw Strauss's *Rosenkavalier* a few months before the murder of the Archduke. Stravinsky outraged Paris with his 'Rite of the Spring' in which, for those who could hear, the age's flirtation with violence was given a voice. Five years earlier, Picasso, a Spaniard living in France, had painted his 'Demoiselles d'Avignon', the first Cubist picture. The air rang with the slogans of artistic clans: Cubists clustered in the Dôme at Montparnasse, exerting a spell over foreigners like Klee, who suffered a conversion in Delaunay's studio and went back to Berlin ablaze with missionary zeal. Between the capitals— especially Paris, Berlin and Munich—ideas and art-dealers shuttled.

In Florence, Marinetti announced the birth of Futurism and dedicated it to war and conflict. 'There is no longer any beauty apart from strife, any masterpiece that is not aggressive.'

There was no lack of voices in every country to shepherd this new craze for violence into respectable paths.

It was unfortunate that the peoples of Europe had not arrived each at the same time at political maturity; more unfortunate that some of them, in that summer of 1914, still felt deprived of assets becoming to their dignity.

Germany had grown up to be the most powerful state between the North Sea and the Niemen yet was by the accident of history denied her due share in the colonial sunshine. It was useless to argue that the patches of colour on Mercator's projection meant very little. And nobody could expect to make a deep impression on the Germans by quoting what a Frenchman said derisively about the French colonies: 'They speak pompously of our African empire and, indeed, only one thing is lacking, the possibility of living there.'

Every year there were 800,000 Germans more than the year before. Germany need only be patient, as Jules Cambon remarked, 'and await the results of the growing birth-rate to dominate Central Europe without a struggle'. But this obvious truth was something that the Germans could not be made to see. Patience is, of all virtues, the hardest for a soaring and confident nation to acquire.

Besides, Central Europe was not big enough for Germany's

ambitions. Possessing the most powerful army on earth, the Germans looked with envy at Britain's navy. If Germany had an instrument like that in her hands might she not have the keys of the world? The hammers clanged furiously in the German dockyards. And the British, at first displeased, were soon alarmed.

'Fritz,' said Prince Henry of Prussia, the Kaiser's brother, one night in 1910 in the equerries' room in Buckingham Palace, 'why is it we cannot get on?'

Sir Frederick Ponsonby, whom he had addressed, spoke of the naughty newspapers, of trade rivalry and so forth.

'No, Fritz,' said the Prince, 'that won't do.'

Ponsonby then said that as the German fleet was not meant to fight France or Russia, it must be meant to fight Britain. The Prince retorted that Germany did not mean to remain for ever at Britain's mercy and subject to British dictation in any European dispute.

Two years—and many ships—later the British Liberal Government of Asquith sent its Secretary of State for War, Lord Haldane, to Berlin. Haldane, a subtle Scots lawyer who remembered with affection his months of study at Göttingen, was a good choice for the mission.[1] But when he proposed an Anglo-German naval agreement which would perpetuate Britain's superiority at sea he could make no progress. He threw in the suggestion that, as a reward, Germany should receive some colonial concessions in Africa, at the expense of Portugal, Britain's ally, who was not informed of the proposal. The bait was not taken.

The Germans asked if Britain would, in exchange for a German naval limitation, promise to be neutral in a European conflict involving France, with whom Britain had a diplomatic entente. The promise could not be given, for the entente with France was on a different footing from that with Portugal.

The British decided that the Germans were interested only in

1. Haldane spoke German, but Richard von Kühlmann, German Chancellor in 1918, said that Bonar Law spoke better German.

holding Britain off while they struck France down, after which they would turn on the rival at sea. The Germans saw the matter differently: Britain, buying at bargain rates a continuance of her command of the seas, would remain able to intervene in a continental war at some moment which she could choose.

Haldane went back to London to report the failure of a mission which was certainly too narrowly conceived and probably too easily discouraged. In another task he had succeeded: that of modernizing the British army and creating the Territorial force. The outcome of his patient exertions, spread over seven years, was shown when the British army, utterly discredited in the Boer War, was revealed in the autumn of 1914 as the finest army of its size in the world.

Opposing him in the Berlin talks, embodying all the enthusiasm of the German masses for their new navy, was the half Englishman who sat on the German throne. Kaiser Wilhelm II was gifted and even brilliant; neurotic and impulsive; easily alarmed yet capable of screwing up his courage. There was a feminine streak in him that sought admiration and caressing words—that had once been captivated by the effusive ways of Philip zu Eulenburg, whose career had come to so deplorable an end twelve years after Wilde's.[1]

1. Philip zu Eulenburg, a Prussian nobleman, sang sweetly and encouraged in the Kaiser the dream of a delightful Richard Coeur-de-Lion/Blondel relationship. He was a master of the tactful gesture and the gushing phrase ('the dear Emperor was suffering terribly, poor fellow . . . I could only catch his dear hand and press it.'). In 1902, announcing himself a broken, dying man (d. 1921), he resigned as ambassador in Vienna and was given a princedom and the Black Eagle. Four years later the sinister Baron Holstein decided that he owed to Eulenburg his dismissal from the Foreign Office. Maximilian Harden, editor of the *Zukunft*, then launched a bold and increasingly frank campaign against Eulenburg, who 'has provided for all his friends. One Moltke is Chief of the General Staff. Another, who is much closer to him, is Commandant of Berlin . . . all good men, musical, poetic.' Harden sought to damage the Kaiser through his friend. While on holiday in the eighties at Starnberg in Bavaria, Eulenburg had shown some partiality for a young fisherman, Jacob Ernst. This individual now testified against him. Eulenburg was tried for perjury, but owing to his breakdown in health, the case was never concluded.

A side of Wilhelm was akin to Ludwig of Bavaria, without the taste. He could be a delightful companion; he could also be rude and overbearing. '*Garçon mal élevé*,' said one royal gentleman, a Tsar, '*et de mauvaise foi*.' Perhaps there had been too many gruff but servile military tutors when he was growing up. 'A bounder,' his English relatives decided. But who was to say whether Wilhelm got his boisterous ways from his Hanoverian mother or his Hohenzollern father? The manners of his uncle, Edward VII, had not been beyond reproach.

The haggard, nervous face of this strange man with the crippled left arm dominated Europe as did no other image of the time. The face, and the voice too. He made 577 public speeches in seventeen years. The Kaiser had a dangerous gift for the phrases that men wanted to hear. In an election the imperial demagogue would probably have been voted President of Germany.

He was not a statesman, not a man of action. He was certainly not a playboy. He was, in some degree, a clown. He did not have the patience to read long state documents. Yet, as a God-fearing Lutheran prince, conscious that he enjoyed the special favour of heaven, he would listen for hours, and with evident pleasure, to sermons which tested the wakefulness of the most insomniac toadies in Potsdam.

He was not sure of himself, although he had a profound self-knowledge which in emergencies came to his rescue. It saved him, for instance, from attempting seriously a task for which he was unsuited—ruling the German Empire. He had one obstinate interest, the sea.

'When I was a little boy,' he told his chancellor one day at Kiel in 1907, 'I was allowed to visit Plymouth and Portsmouth with kind aunts and friendly admirals. I admired the proud English ships in those harbours. Then there awoke in me the desire to build ships of my own like these.'

But to say that his passionate addiction to his navy was a mere whim, a childish, petulant fancy, is not to be just. The navy was to be his own historic memorial, as the Empire had been Bismarck's. It would be his way of laying to rest that envy of England which tormented him, the rejected half-brother of the British family. It would be his way of proving that Queen Victoria's favourite grandson was her truest heir.

There was perhaps more in it than that. The sea, alike as symbol and reality, was his path of escape from the Germany which he only partly liked, from the Prussia which was so grim, so constricting—like a woollen vest, as Bismarck said, 'it scratches but it keeps you warm'. Wilhelm had a sensitive skin. And he was perhaps more of an Englishman than he knew. By sea he could reach the Mediterranean sun, the Baltic horizons, the dark magnificence of the Norwegian fjords. Conscious of talents, of a profound maladjustment in his life, a futility which was not appeased by the uniforms he changed ten times a day, Wilhelm satisfied at sea some deep need for fulfilment. Fulfilment or liberation?

So the imperial Daimler Benz would play the Siegfried motif from the 'Ring' at every street crossing on the way to the station where the train stood that would take the traveller to Kiel. There the *Hohenzollern* would already be getting steam up. Ahead lay empty, salt-stung days, and, in the evenings, jovial, obsequious sessions of the Moselle Club—or, if it was Sunday, some Lutheran sermons. It was all comforting to a restless, divided, incurably romantic man.

If the growing German navy corresponded to some psychological need in its all-highest master it also corresponded to an urge for self-assertion in the German people. At the slightest suggestion that the size of its fleet should be limited Germany broke out in a pandemonium of hostility. It was almost as impossible to suggest a cut in the naval estimates as to propose that Alsace-Lorraine, prize of the glorious victory of 1870, might be handed back to France or, at least, given autonomy.

Between Germany and France lay those two provinces, never likely to be an occasion of war, yet barring the way to peace and reconciliation.

In January 1913 Raymond Poincaré, son of Lorraine, was elected President of France. As the retiring President Fallières left the palace, it is said that he remarked to his Prime Minister, 'I greatly fear that war is entering the Elysée after me.'[1]

But Poincaré was not a war-monger. He was simply another of those who believed that war was inevitable. Believing that, he devoted himself to ensuring that France would be in as favourable a strategic position as possible in meeting that which could not be avoided.

He was a man of ferocious industry and punctilious honesty. Imagination was denied to him; passion was not. To the depths of his being he resented as an outrage, a crime against nature, the tearing of Alsace and Lorraine from the sacred body of France. That one day they should be reunited was the most desirable thing in the world. That this could happen only after a war he was realist enough to see.

The idea that was entertained became in time the master of the dwelling. Preparing against war, by stroke after stroke of policy, Poincaré deepened the ditch which divided Europe in two: France and Russia on one side with perhaps Britain; Germany and Austria on the other with—but this was less likely—Italy.

He denied Austria access to the Paris Bourse for a loan. He insisted that a 'weak' French ambassador at St. Petersburg should be supplanted, first by Delcassé, a man consumed with a desire to avenge himself on Germany for having brought about his dismissal in 1905, and later by Maurice Paléologue, an acute if flamboyant professional diplomat who was the President's creature.

A series of torchlight military parades was promoted through French cities, exciting the enthusiasm of the people for their army. All this had a certain effect when acting upon a public, which, in Paris at least, was already trifling with thoughts of glory. In 1912 an observer of the young men at the Sorbonne had noticed: 'War—the word has acquired a sudden prestige.'

The term of military service was lengthened from two years to three—200,000 young men kept another year from production

1. This anecdote is reported by Joseph Caillaux, a fiercely anti-Poincaré witness, and must be regarded with caution.

and not one soldier more in time of war, as Joseph Caillaux acidly observed. However, Maurice Paléologue had come all the way from St. Petersburg to announce that the Russians insisted on the change.

In constant attendance on Poincaré was the Russian ambassador, Alexander Isvolski, a corrupt but intelligent man, a provincial Russian noble who insisted on speaking French at home and was intensely vain and snobbish. He was married to the pretty half-German Countess Toll, known as '*le sourire de Paris*'. Isvolski had the appearance and the unforgiving nature of a Tartar. About him there clung a perpetual odour of Parma violets.

Since 1908 this man's undeviating malice had been aimed at Austria, whose Foreign Minister at that time, Count Aerenthal, had tricked him. Aerenthal had appeared to agree to a modification of the convention which forbade Russian warships to pass through the Dardanelles. In return Isvolski had half-consented to an Austrian annexation of Bosnia. A fortnight later Bosnia was annexed by Austria. But when Isvolski tried to win the freedom of the Dardanelles for Russian ships he found himself baulked by the veto of Britain and was given no comfort in Berlin. He resigned from his post as Russian Foreign Minister and gave himself up to thoughts of vengeance: '*Le sale juif m'a trompé*.' Aerenthal was of Jewish origin.

Poincaré and Isvolski were not likely to encourage each other in schemes for European pacification.

In the French President's speeches there was an undercurrent of menace which stopped short of provocation but reminded the world that he was the head of a nation that meant to be respected. The Paris newspapers gave him their applause. Those newspapers deserve some attention.

In February 1905 one M. de Verneuil, a leading Paris stockbroker, warned the Russian Prime Minister, Count Witte, that there would be a disastrous fall in Russian funds on the Bourse unless—'The press exists. It is a force. It will make you realize this if you do not act.' In short, Count Witte should spend two or three million francs in bribing the Paris newspapers to support the diplomatic or financial interests of the Russian government. Witte took the advice, distributing the money through Arthur Raffalovitch, adviser to the Tsarist Ministry of Finance. The *Temps* was bought, the *Matin* was bought. Almost every newspaper in Paris was bought. 'Every day', said Raffalovitch, 'one learns to despise someone else.'

Witte, who was already paying out 100,000 francs a month in bribes, agreed to pay another 250,000 francs (£10,000) a month. These subventions continued with the full knowledge of the French government in Poincaré's time. They were used to advance causes which both the Russian and French governments had at heart. For instance, the three years' military service law. 'Klotz asks for a second slice,' Raffalovitch told St. Petersburg: 'a big press campaign is needed for the vote on the military law.' Sazonov, the Russian Foreign Minister, made support for the law a condition for continuing the press subsidies. The press responded nobly.

'War', wrote Paul Bourget in the *Echo de Paris*, 'is truly regenerating, adorned by that seduction which the eternal bellicose instinct has reawakened in the hearts of men.'

The situation was therefore this: the thrifty French people supplied Russia with their savings—enough to pay the entire cost to Russia of her disastrous war against Japan. Some modest percentage of this money was then used, with the French government's connivance, to bribe important sections of the Paris press in favour of the eternal bellicose instinct which, left to themselves, the level-headed peasants of France would have found less seductive!

Over this malodorous terrain Poincaré, a man of the utmost personal probity, pursued his inflexible course.

Through force of character and political cunning he had been able to stretch his constitutional powers and establish a personal ascendancy over the French government. For instance, during that summer of 1914 he prevailed on Aristide Briand, one of his ministers, not to visit Kiel for the regatta, insisting that the trip would be displeasing to Russia. In fact, the Prince of Monaco, who was to be Briand's host, had intended to bring Wilhelm and the Frenchman together. To Poincaré, curator of the brittle architecture of European diplomacy, such a meeting was alarming and offensive.

On the other side of the great divide a spirit as bitter and narrow as his laboured to prevent the solution of another dangerous European problem.

Among the 7,000,000 Magyars of Hungary there were 800,000 nobles, of higher or lower degree. The leader of this proud and arrogant caste was Count Stephen Tisza, Prime Minister of Hungary, a man with three ruling passions: the Bible, politics and horses. Once he had been a famous dancer of the czardas. Once he had preached in the churches of his creed. Once he had bred beautiful horses and ridden wildly on the puszta. Now in his middle fifties, this harsh, charmless and compelling man had given himself up to a dual task: to maintain the Habsburg monarchy and to preserve his own people, the Magyar nobility, as dominant partners in the Austrian Empire. To this mission he brought a steely courage and a fierce religious belief. Tisza was a Calvinist of the Calvinists, pupil of a famous Calvinist school at Debreczen, and not without a tincture of the fanaticism which that faith sometimes engenders. He knew Austria to be feckless; France he believed to be decadent. In English life Parliament and the London clubs appealed to him. Germany, strong and dutiful, he admired.

The 'Bible man' was implacably opposed to any political advancement of Austria's Slav subjects. For instance, to erect the southern Slavs of Croatia and Bosnia into a third kingdom of the Dual Monarchy would be to reduce Hungary's prestige. In addition, it would encourage inconvenient dreams of freedom among Hungary's Rumanians in Transylvania. Tisza wanted things preserved as they were: an Austrian emperor who also sat on the throne of Hungary; the dependent Slavs kept in their place; and no more Slavs brought into the empire. The Hungarian Count Andrassy had put the matter concisely to an Austrian colleague: 'Take care of your barbarians, we will take care of ours.'

But the simple formula which satisfied men like Tisza ignored Slav nationalism, for ever boiling up in the Balkans, and threatening to disrupt from below the dry old crust of Austrian imperialism. Serving as the spearhead of this Slav revolutionary spirit were the Serbs, encouraged, advised and supplied from the fountainhead of all pan-Slav enthusiasm, holy mother Russia herself.

One man in a position of authority in Austria had seen the danger of a completely negative policy towards the Slav problem, the Archduke Franz Ferdinand, heir to the throne and commander-in-chief of the army, a man who had more than his share of the faults of the disastrous Habsburg brood. Every now and then he would be overcome by paroxysms of rage—products of the disease he had contracted—the seats of railway carriages were ripped by his sabre, or an incautious beater was shot at one of the game drives he was for ever attending. A few months before the crime at Sarajevo the Archduke had killed his 5000th stag; the walls of country houses all over Europe were adorned with antlers he had graciously slain and bequeathed. Even for a Habsburg he was notably unpopular in Vienna, and more so in Budapest.

But the Archduke had more political realism than the rest of his clan. In a cloudy way he saw that the Habsburgs, having for so long justified their privileges as champions of Christendom against the Turk, needed a new *raison d'être* now that the Turk was manifestly in full retreat. He dreamt of a federation of kingdoms, Croat and perhaps Bohemian, as well as Austrian and Hungarian, all united under an emperor.[1] His ideas, vague as they might be, were anathema alike to the Serbs, to the Magyars and to the Russians. These ideas perished with the Archduke at Sarajevo.

From that moment onwards there was little chance of a peaceful evolution of the Austrian Empire: either the subject Slavs would be kept by force in the place of inferiority which Providence had

1. A few weeks before his death, the Archduke agreed with the Kaiser in opposing a war with Serbia—'All we would get would be a pack of thieves, ruffians, murderers and a few plum trees.'

assigned to them or they would win by rebellion their freedom from the stony-hearted old despot in the Palace of Schönbrunn. The first meant that in all probability Austria would come to depend more and more on German military and political support. As for the second possibility, it was a steady light burning, like a lamp before an ikon, in the murk of Russian policy.

Inside Austria there was precious little pan-Slav feeling. The Croats, who were Catholics, disliked the Serbs, who longed to incorporate them in a Greater—and Orthodox—Serbia. Neither Croats nor Serbs had much in common with the Czechs, a thriving, enlightened people who had, at their head, a man of luminous intelligence, Thomas Masaryk. Nor did the Czechs, whether Catholic or Hussite in religion, look with brotherly admiration upon Holy Orthodox Russia, sunk in superstition, ignorance and squalor, governed by the blackest reactionaries in Christendom and for ever bearing in its lineaments the threat of anarchy. Compared with Russia's unfathomable muddle and corruption, the mere incompetence of Austrian rule shone with something like administrative genius.

Yet there was a magnetism about Russia—the appeal exerted by its vastness; the vitality of its people among whom 2,500,000 births were recorded each year; their hardiness and patriotism. That 'cold Orient', as a German called it, teemed with life and sparkled with hints of surprises to come.

Russia had two main purposes in national policy: to break out through the Dardanelles into the Mediterranean, and to bring the Slav peoples of the Balkans firmly under the wing of St. Petersburg. This second purpose made a particularly strong appeal to educated Russians. The pan-Slav doctrine was given its most precise shape by N. J. Danielevski who proposed that, under Russian influence, there should be a federation of kingdoms— Czecho-Slovak; Serb-Croat-Slovene; Bulgarian; Rumanian; Greek; Hungarian; with a 'province of Constantinople' thrown in. Ninety-three years after this Slav vision was first conjured up, a glance at the map suggests that Danielevski was not without prescience.

Thus when the Russian secret service deployed roubles, agents, intrigues and propaganda among the Slavs of Austria and Hungary it was forwarding a cause that the people of Russia approved. There would never be friendship between Russia and Austria so long as Slavs in the Balkans owed allegiance to Vienna.

As for the Dardanelles project, that dream of blue water haunting the Russian soul traversed a German project of a different kind.

Since 1902 a German consortium financed by the Deutsche Bank had been creating a railway system in Asia Minor. The line pushed out south and east from Constantinople towards Baghdad and Basra. The idea of a railway linking the Mediterranean and the Persian Gulf had occurred as early as 1830 to a young British officer, Francis Chesney. One day in 1899 Cecil Rhodes suggested to the Kaiser that Germany might find an outlet in Asia Minor for her pent-up national energies. The Kaiser, on a visit to Constantinople in 1898, dazzled the Turkish Sultan Abdul Hamid into granting a railway concession to a German company called 'La Société Impériale Ottomane du Chemin de Fer de Baghdad'. When Britain, France and Russia refused their financial participation, Dr. von Gwinner and Dr. Siemens raised the money from native German sources. By 1914, £12,000,000 had been spent and the railway had reached Nusaybin on what is now the border of Syria. Another 600 miles of construction would carry it to Baghdad and Basra. In all, the Germans would control a railway network 2375 miles long, linked with German-owned railways in the Balkans.

Naturally such an enormous conception had political and military significance. The elder Moltke, mapping in Turkey as a young officer, had dreamed long ago of a German dominion over the crumbling Turkish Empire. Dr. Grothe, a pan-German publicist, said, 'Anatolia, like the Baghdad railway, must belong to Germany.' In 1902 Dr. Rohrbach, a busy exponent of the project, rejoiced: 'The railway under the control of the Deutsche Bank is a German enterprise. . . . England can be attacked and mortally wounded by land only in one place, Egypt. But Turkey

37

can never recover Egypt until she is mistress of a developed railway system.'

Before the last section of the railway from Baghdad to the Gulf could be built, Britain had to be placated. Thirteen days before the Archduke Franz Ferdinand was murdered, an Anglo-German agreement covering the question was initialled in London.

The German trend towards the East, of which the Baghdad railway was the most dramatic expression, ran athwart Russia's ambitions in the Balkans and the Dardanelles. The lines of fate of the two empires crossed at Constantinople.

The troubles of Europe in the summer of 1914 were serious but curable. Time was needed: time, patience and a reasonable allowance of diplomatic skill. Time was, perhaps, running short. The Germans had drawn on their national capital to the tune of £53,000,000 by a special tax to finance military spending. They had added 136,000 officers and men to their peace-time army. The French, by the Three Years' Service Law, had made an inroad on their manpower resources the advantage of which, by its nature, could only be temporary. Everywhere the soldiers watched the hands of a clock which moved steadily nearer zero hour.

But among the politicians there was a notable tendency to shrink from final reckonings. Russia did not propose to fight for the Straits. France was not likely to launch a war for the recovery of Alsace-Lorraine. One day in June the British settled their long dispute with the Germans over the Baghdad Railway. Might not other irritations yield to treatment? Given time, given patience, the German taxpayer might one day rebel against paying for the Kaiser's fleet. It was an ace which the British taxpayer, however reluctantly, was always going to trump. The Emperor Franz Joseph could not live for ever and when he died his Slav subjects might hope for better things.

Short of some appalling mischance, it seemed that Europe

would be able to lurch unsteadily on her course, and if mischance befell there was surely enough good sense and goodwill among her statesmen to interrupt a chain reaction of violence. Only a conjunction of the stars, utterly improbable and extraordinarily malign, could bring about a catastrophe. But were the statesmen alert enough? Did they have the active, resourceful and passionate desire for peace which, in an emergency, might be needed? Was the network of negotiation linking the six main centres of European power capable of the speed which, in a frantic and confused crisis, would maintain the sanity of rulers? These questions were soon to be answered.

In the meantime, families prepared for the seashore or the mountains. Spades and pails were mobilized and lodgings sought. In the fields the peasants sharpened their scythes and prepared to gather in the harvest: the wheat, oats, barley, rye and maize on which Europe would live until spring returned. Staff officers sitting in their offices followed the progress of the harvest as if on it depended the sounding of a signal, the setting of an alarm.

'S'il est entré dans l'histoire c'est bien
malgré lui'—
ALFRED DUMAINE, *La Dernière
Ambassade*

3

A Stroll in the Park at Potsdam

'BERCHTOLD pleases me,' said the Emperor Franz Joseph.
'I have given him my confidence. That is sufficient.' Alas,
it was not sufficient.

With his charm, his social gifts, Leopold, Count Berchtold
von und zu Ungarisch, had made a soothing impression on the
old man. He was a gentleman, wealthy, the owner of an imposing
castle in Moravia, surrounded by magnificent forests. His wife,
born a Karolyi, had brought him valuable property in Hungary.
He became a Hungarian by law: he sometimes wore, to the
delight of Viennese ladies, the costume of a Magyar nobleman
with unusually splendid fur on his dolman, and a heron's plume
fastened by jewels to his head-dress. He even made efforts to
learn the Hungarian language.

How happy Count Berchtold might have been had he been

left to manage his estates (which he did well enough), to run his horses at the Vienna racecourses, and to loiter in the antique shops of the cities he visited. He was a cultivated man who asked for little more from life but the pleasures which great wealth, good taste and a frivolous disposition can contrive. Duty called him in another direction. His father-in-law insisted that he should become a diplomat and one day the Emperor commanded him to be Foreign Minister. So there he was, the nominal master of the ochre-grey palace in the Ballhausplatz in Vienna, directing the tortuous mental processes which passed for the foreign policy of the Austrian Empire.

For this task Count Berchtold had neither the aptitude nor the will. About his distinguished person there clung the aroma of an immense melancholy—the melancholy of a man who knew that his shoulders were unsuited to the burden laid upon them. To escape from the disagreeable sense that he was miscast, the Count took refuge in the lighter society of Vienna: discreet restaurants, little theatres of the suburbs, where a high dignitary of the empire, to whom the Hofburg was open, whose wife, as one entitled to wear the 'starred cross', was admitted to state balls even without her husband, could permissibly amuse himself.

In Vienna, the Emperor Franz Joseph, once married to an impossible wife, the head of an impossible clan, ruled over an impossible empire from his audience chamber in the Hofburg. With its Spanish court, its German nobility and its brilliant Jews the city was at once cosmopolitan and provincial. It lay on the far borders of the West. 'Asia', Metternich had said, 'begins on the Hauptstrasse-Landstrasse.' Irony, charm and the odour of decay hung over the city.

There were two social sets. There was the aristocratic clan, intensely interwoven by marriage, all cousins, all calling one another *du*; pious and trivial, living for gossip, without a single intellectual interest; the women good-natured and inclined to run to fat. And there was the smart set, on whom respectable people frowned and who did not go to court. One or two families, like the Rothschilds, dwelling in their palaces in Theresianumgasse and Prinz Eugen Strasse, bridged the two societies. But in neither set, in none of the drawing-rooms where the ladies smoked cigars and talked scandal, was it noticed that intelligent, charming, clever Count Berchtold was not equal to his task. Others were harsher in their judgement. 'Every elegance, good manners, and that is all' was the verdict of a Rumanian politician. Thomas Masaryk, the austere Czech patriot, spoke contemptuously of the care that Berchtold lavished on his choice of hats and ties.

So the belief has grown up that the Austrian Foreign Minister was a worthless person. But what can be said against Berchtold? That he owned racehorses? So did Lord Rosebery. That he was a dandy? So was Caillaux. That he liked pretty women? So did M. Clemenceau. That he served his master reluctantly? No more so than Moltke. Let one quality, too, be conceded to this Austrian nobleman with the disdainful manner: he was sincerely devoted to the country he served disastrously and with all the wisdom he could muster.

On the day of the murder at Sarajevo the Foreign Minister hurried back to Vienna from his castle at Buchlau. Ready to greet him at the Ballhausplatz was Count Forgach, a diplomat of marked strength of character, who was filled with hatred of the Serbs. And the god of war himself was on the way: General Conrad von Hötzendorff had telegraphed the Emperor, 'Shall I march on Vienna?' He was told to march.

There followed a series of intense consultations at the Ballhausplatz. An unexampled crisis of prestige and authority had arisen in Austria. The heir to the throne and his wife had been murdered and there was good ground for believing that this crime, which was also an affront, had been inspired and perhaps planned by influences domiciled in Serbia.

At that moment Austria held all the moral cards in her hand. One of the extraordinary features in the developing crisis is how badly these cards were played and how swiftly they lost their value. Indeed, it seems that the Austrians hardly understood that the moral issues in the case had any political importance at all.

They allowed seven days to pass before making their first definite diplomatic move, and that a secret one. How much indignation had evaporated in that week!

What was to be done? Conrad was from the start the evangelist of preventive war. He was an officer out of some satirical play, with fierce, upswept moustaches and simple warlike views. For fourteen years he had kept at the head of counter-espionage one Colonel Redl, who sold all Austria's military secrets to the Russians. Redl said, ungratefully, of his patron, 'Believe me, he is a poor judge of men.' Forgach, the professional Serb-hater, also urged war as a solution. By 29 June Berchtold was won over to the idea. At first he thought that it would be sufficient to invade Serbia with troops on a peace footing. Conrad disillusioned him. To do that would throw the machinery of mobilization out of gear: reservists would arrive at their depots and find no skeleton units to absorb them, train schedules would be thrown into confusion, etc., etc. In Vienna, as later in St. Petersburg and Berlin, the militarists guarded their mobilization plans like anxious nurses watching over a delicate infant.

Count Tisza, the intransigent Prime Minister of Hungary, summoned from Budapest, alone held out for caution, for some form of punishment to be inflicted on Serbia which would fall short of open conflict. Tisza feared that war with Serbia might bring about war with Russia—Cossacks pouring into Transylvania to free its Rumanian population from their Magyar masters! Even if victory came, could one trust Berchtold, that weakling whose measure Tisza had taken long ago, not to add Serbs to Austria's Slav subjects? On this point Berchtold's words were and remained equivocal. Behind the words lay a covert purpose: to break the Serbian kingdom into fragments, distributing so much to Albania and Bulgaria while keeping a modest portion of the booty for Austria herself.

For Franz Joseph's advisers one question was swiftly revealed as dominant: would Austria's ally Germany show herself ready to march if Russian armies moved to the support of Serbia?

Conrad thought he knew the answer. A few weeks before, he

43

had talked with Moltke, the German Chief of Staff, at Carlsbad. The German had argued in favour of an early war: 'Every delay means a lessening of our chances. It is impossible to compete with Russia in numbers.' But that was in May, in peace. Would it hold good in July, when the clouds were already beginning to show above the southern horizon? Conrad had no illusions about Moltke's fitness for desperate deeds and stern enterprises. Besides, it was necessary to hear the views of the All-Highest War Lord himself, who in a day or two would be leaving for Kiel for his annual cruise off the Norwegian coast.

A personal letter to the Kaiser was drafted, signed by Franz Joseph and taken to Berlin on 4 July by Count Hoyos, the head of Berchtold's private office and an enthusiastic partisan of war. In its concluding passage the letter said that there could be no reconciliation between Austria and Serbia, which must be 'eliminated as a political power-factor in the Balkans'. In effect, the letter asked for German approval of an Austrian attack on Serbia.

It found the Kaiser in a confident and chivalrous mood, mindful of what he owed in honour to a venerable fellow-emperor, mindful too of his friendship with the murdered man. A knightly gesture was appropriate—and was all the more appealing since it seemed unlikely that anything more than words would be called for. Already he had rebuked his ambassador in Vienna, who smugly reported that he had urged caution on the Austrians.

The Kaiser did not think that the Tsar, limp little Nikky, would take the side of the regicides; more important, the German General Staff did not believe that the Russians were ready for war. They lacked the artillery. Their strategic railway system was far from complete.

On 5 July the Kaiser went for a stroll in the park at Potsdam with his chancellor, that bearded, sad-eyed giant Theobald von Bethmann Hollweg, whom irreverent young officers called 'Lanky Theobald', and Under-Secretary Zimmerman of the Foreign Office. By the time the walk was over, the Kaiser had made up his mind.

Not another man had been consulted. The Foreign Minister was on his honeymoon and had not been recalled. The experienced, too subtle, too slippery ex-chancellor Bernhard von Bülow had not been called in. There in the park with Bethmann Hollweg, whose judgement he despised, and Zimmerman, an official, the Kaiser reached his decision. He told the Austrian ambassador in Berlin that Germany would cover Austria should Russia intervene.

Calling the War Minister, General Falkenhayn, to his presence, the Kaiser said that an Austrian note to Serbia might have serious consequences, and put the question, Was the German army ready for any eventuality? Falkenhayn clicked his heels, brought his hand smartly to his helmet and replied, 'Completely, Your Majesty.' The last touches to the army's mobilization plans had been made on the last day of March. The Kaiser asked representatives of big business if they were ready for war. They told him they must have a fortnight to sell their foreign securities. Fortified by these assurances, the Kaiser left for his northern cruise, as he had planned, next morning at quarter past nine. At Kiel he saw Krupp at dinner on the yacht and told him that if Russia mobilized he would declare war at once: 'No one will be able to reproach me again with want of resolution.'

Probably he did not believe that Austria would ever go to war with Serbia. Russia? An empire that could hardly keep its balance in peace, far less conduct a war. Nothing in that quarter need trouble a man to whom the sea was calling! As for the remoter contingencies—France, for ever resentful; Britain, never to be trusted—they were too nebulous to be thought of. Wilhelm went off on the *Hohenzollern* with the good conscience of one who had given his hand to a comrade entering a just quarrel. What less could a Christian monarch do?

In fact, however, the Kaiser had, on a generous impulse, handed over German policy to the keeping of any adventurer, fool or firebrand, whether called Conrad or Berchtold, who might gain the ascendancy in the Vienna Cabinet. If the Austrians decided to gamble at the tables they knew from that moment onwards that they did so with a German banker behind them. The walk in the park at Potsdam had taken the strollers farther than they realized.

Exultant, Hoyos went back to Vienna and reported to the Emperor. 'Now we can no longer turn back,' said the old man. 'It will be a terrible war.'

Franz Joseph had been won round to the war party by the argument that to falter in action at this moment would appear cowardly to the Germans.

And now the last barrier gave way—Tisza surrendered. There was something in the Calvinist soul of that harsh Hungarian noble that recoiled from war. As he wrote to a niece he was fond of: 'War even if victorious is terrible. For my soul every war means misery, anguish, devastation.' When he drove back to Budapest after the decisive Cabinet meeting he was cheered by peasants in a village. 'If only they knew how little I deserve their cheers!' he said grimly. Like the Emperor, he had probably been won over to the cause he distrusted so deeply by the fear that any sign of shrinking on Austria's part might cause the Germans to dismiss her as unworthy of alliance.

Newspapers in Vienna and Budapest faithfully echoed the hardening of resolution among the politicians. On 2 July the *Pester Lloyd* was protesting against the mere idea of a campaign of revenge against the Serbs; in Vienna the *Freie Presse* dismissed wars of revenge as out of the question. By 14 July the first newspaper had become violently anti-Serb, while the second was 'appealing to the sword of the veterans'.

In his room in the Foreign Ministry, looking over the horse-chestnut trees of the Burgplatz to the equestrian statue of Archduke Charles, Alexander Musulin, head of Chancery in the Austrian Foreign Office, set to work on the task assigned to him: devising an ultimatum which Serbia could not accept.

In fact, Austria had an even better case against the Serbian government than she realized. She believed that responsibility for the Sarajevo murders lay with the Narodna Obrana (National Defence Society), a revolutionary association with a following among Bosnian students. The truth was different and more damaging to the good name of Serbia.

In the first days of June two young men, Princip and Cabrinovitch, had slipped across the River Drina from Serbia into Bosnia. They were armed with bombs and pistols. These, like their mission, had been given them by the Black Hand, a Serbian terrorist organization at the head of which was a burly Serb colonel, Dragutin Dimitrievitch, who was also head of the Intelligence Service of the Serbian General Staff.

The Black Hand was Dimitrievitch's own personal contribution to the Balkan pattern of violence. He was brave, vain, unbalanced and ruthless. The Black Hand bore the marks of its founder's imagination. Its proceedings were shrouded in lurid melodrama and its real name was 'Union or Death'—the political union of all the Serbians: the death of those who stood in the way of this aim or of the martyrs who were willing to give their lives to accomplish it. The symbol of the society was a death's head, a banner, dagger, bomb and poison glass, indicating plainly enough the desperate repertory of methods by which the Black Hand was prepared to pursue its ends. A candidate for membership was initiated in a darkened room in Belgrade where he stood before a black-draped table and took the oath by sun and earth, by God, honour and life.

The Black Hand was strong enough to challenge the Serbian government in its own capital. In the spring of 1914 Protitch, the Minister of the Interior, had closed the society's premises and had mustered a large force of gendarmes in readiness for a trial of strength. But the Black Hand had powerful friends. Hartwig, the Russian minister, intervened and the order against the Black Hand was rescinded.

The Russian military attaché in Belgrade, Colonel Victor Artmanov, was, from an early stage, a party to the Black Hand conspiracy to murder the Archduke. After consulting higher authority in St. Petersburg, perhaps the Minister of War, Sukhomlinov, perhaps one of the Grand Dukes, Artmanov had told Dimitrievitch: 'Go ahead. If attacked, you will not stand alone.'

When the Central Committee of the Black Hand met in the offices of the Serb General Staff, Artmanov gave the conspirators his assurance that, whatever happened, Russia would lend Serbia her support. Soon afterwards Artmanov prudently left Serbia for a period of six weeks. Later he claimed that he had heard of the Sarajevo outrage while in Zürich.

The assassination was, therefore, something graver than an irresponsible conspiracy among a group of young fanatics.

The conduct of the Serbian Prime Minister, Nicholas Pasitch, must also be noted. This tall, good-looking man, whose dignified beard and imposing presence disguised one of the cunningest foxes in the Balkans, knew about the projected murder almost as soon as it was planned. Perhaps he heard about it accidentally, through some eavesdropper in one of the handful of Belgrade cafés where politics was discussed. More likely, an agent of his, a railway clerk named Gaginovitch, who was also a member of the Black Hand, passed the news on to him.

Pasitch told his Minister of the Interior he would order the frontier authorities to stop the intending assassins. Unfortunately, the order arrived too late, or the frontier officers were themselves members of the Black Hand. Pasitch then instructed the Serbian minister in Vienna, Jovan Jovanovitch, to give a warning to the Austrian government.

Here two dilemmas were present together. Pasitch did not dare to act against the Black Hand because he was himself afraid of them. And Jovanovitch could not transmit the warning in too precise a form lest he betray the truth that his government knew more than it ought to know about a murder plot hatched in its own territory and, indeed, in one of its own offices. Instead of going to Berchtold, with whom he was on the worst of terms, he went to von Bilinski, the Austrian Finance Minister, and spoke in guarded and evasive phrases about the Archduke's reported intention to take command at army manœuvres in Bosnia:

'The Serbs must regard this as an act of provocation. . . . Among the Serb youths there may be one who will put a ball-cartridge in his rifle in place of a blank, and he may fire it, and the bullet might strike the man giving provocation. Therefore it would be good and reasonable that the Archduke should not go to Sarajevo.'

Put like that, without a scrap of evidence to support it, the observation sounded like a threat or an insulting reflection on the loyalty of Austrian regiments. In any case, it failed in its purpose. Bilinski was on bad terms with the Austrian Prime Minister, a nonentity named Count Sturgkh. He disliked the Archduke Franz Ferdinand. It is quite likely that Jovanovitch's obscure message made no impression on his mind. Whatever the reason, Bilinski did not report the matter to Berchtold. And not one soldier, not one detective, was added to the Archduke's guard.

When the news of the Sarajevo murder reached Pasitch in Belgrade, he stroked his long beard: 'It is bad. It will mean war.' Then he went to bed to think. In the days that followed he did a great deal of thinking but not one step did he take towards launching an investigation of the murder plot. The reason is not far to seek. An investigation would have proved that too many highly placed persons in Belgrade were party to the crime. One of them, in all likelihood, was the Crown Prince-Regent Alexander himself.

The day after the murder three rough-looking individuals, ostentatiously armed, called on the proprietor of the Belgrade newspaper *Balkan*. He would be wise, they told him, to keep his mouth shut about any contacts the murderer Cabrinovitch might have had in the town.

Meanwhile the busy drafters continued with their literary task in Vienna and by 19 July the final text of the ultimatum to Serbia was approved by a Council of Joint Ministers of the Austro-Hungarian Empire. Tisza made Hungary's acceptance conditional on the renunciation by Austria of any conquests in Serbia. Berchtold and the others agreed, cynically assuming that after the victory over Serbia the condition would be a dead letter.

On that day the Kaiser from his yacht ordered Count Wedel, a member of his suite, to warn the North German Lloyd and

Hamburg–Amerika shipping companies that an Austrian ultimatum might be expected in four days' time. On 19 July, too, came the first real break on the Vienna, Berlin and Paris stock exchanges. *The Times* reported 'a keen continental demand for bar gold'.

Delivery of the Austrian document was delayed for a special reason.

> '*St. Petersburg floats like a bark overladen with precious goods while the waves seem as if, deriding her false foundations, they would overturn in a few hours that which the will of man had raised with such untiring labour.*'
>
> Murray's Guide to Russia, 1865

4

The Voyage of M. Poincaré

PRESIDENT POINCARÉ, with his Prime Minister and Foreign Minister Viviani, was taking a trip by sea to St. Petersburg in the cruiser *France*. He arrived off Peterhof, the Tsar's summer home, at lunch-time on the day following the Cabinet meeting in Vienna. He thought that the palace was a rather *fadé* replica of Versailles. Salutes rumbled across the Gulf of Finland. National anthems were played. Poincaré did everything that was expected of a visiting head of state; that is to say, he made an excellent impression at the state banquet and pretended not to notice when the Tsarina had one of her heart attacks. To the imperial couple he handed over the gifts of France: the Gobelins, the gold fittings for the Tsar's motor-car. His experienced eye took in the four charming daughters, the Grand Duchesses Olga, Tatiana, Maria and Anastasia, who, with schoolgirlish delight, accepted the

51

diamond wrist-watches he had brought from Paris. With mixed feelings, M. Poincaré recalled the story Paléologue had told him about the girls and the crapulous monk Rasputin.[1]

Next day the President visited St. Petersburg, unaccompanied by his host, who found his own capital an uncongenial place. Ever since, by persistently rebellious behaviour, his subjects had shown how little they deserved to see their Little Father's countenance, the Tsar had shut himself up in his palaces at Tsarskoe Seloe or Peterhof, the Oriental fantasy in parti-coloured marble which Peter the Great had built on a bluff overlooking the Gulf of Finland. There he lived a quiet suburban life, punishing his ungrateful capital by his absence and enjoying something like safety. It was not achieved without effort.

The life of the Tsar was an expensive concern of the Russian security service. Night and day, Cossacks of the Escort Regiment galloped fifty yards behind one another, along the avenue surrounding the palace at Tsarskoe Seloe. They were, however, only a portion of the security force which protected the Russian sovereign and his family. In addition, the palace gates and sentry-boxes in the parks were manned by His Imperial Majesty's Regiment, 5000 strong, picked from the Guard. A railway regiment of two battalions looked after the imperial train and inspected the permanent way. Police of the Imperial Court (250 men) kept an eye on the entrances to the palace. Should His Imperial Majesty venture outside the palace, say, to bathe in the fjords or to play tennis, his safety was in the keeping of his Personal Police (300 men), a branch of the Ochrana, the Secret Police. This fearsome organization had its headquarters in a low yellow building with barred windows on the Kronversky Prospekt in St. Petersburg.

M. Poincaré came quite near this inconspicuous building on his way through the city. Driving at a fast trot over the Troitski Bridge past the raspberry-coloured British Embassy, he visited the fortress-church of Peter and Paul. He had an escort of

1. Current gossip alleged that Rasputin, on the pretext of blessing the Grand Duchesses, used to treat them with familiarity in bed.

ferocious-looking Cossacks of the Guard in scarlet. Along the route he acknowledged the cheers of the crowd which the police had courteously collected to greet him.

The beautiful city floated on the waters of the Neva where Peter had set it 200 years before, a miracle of Russian genius, daring and power. If there was a nuance of pathos in its muted brilliance there was also a gesture of defiance. Nature, fate and the external world—all were being confronted by the will of the dead Tsar in the capital he had built in marble on the marshes of the Gulf of Finland.

How could one fail to rejoice that such magnificence and such vitality were at France's side! How could one resist the warlike pride and ardour surging up in one's bosom when, on the vast lion-coloured plain of Krasnoe Seloe, three-quarters of an hour outside the city by train, 60,000 troops paraded before the Little Father—and only French marches were played!

While they helped to decorate the tables for dinner, the Grand Duchesses Anastasia and Militza, wives of the Grand Dukes Nicholas and Peter, and devoted daughters of that old adventurer, King Nicholas of Montenegro, surrounded Maurice Paléologue, the French ambassador, with flattering attentions. Their dark eyes sparkled with excitement as they told him: Father[1] says we'll have war before the end of the month. Look at this little box! It has real soil from Lorraine in it. Our armies will meet in Berlin. But I must restrain myself. The Tsar has his eye on me.'

When news filtered through to the French president that there had been disturbances in the industrial quarters of St. Petersburg

1. Nicholas was not, however, as wholehearted in his support of the Russian cause as his daughters may have wished. His was a difficult life just then. He knew that the Serbians meant to swallow up his little mountain kingdom. He hoped, on the one hand, for a Russian subsidy towards the up-keep of his army, at that moment much in arrears of pay—and, on the other hand, for a bribe from Austria. His policy, inevitably tortuous, was complicated by the undisguised partisanship of his subjects for the Serbs. Only a fortnight before Poincaré's arrival at Peterhof, King Nicholas had driven back anti-Austrian demonstrators in his capital by repeated sallies in the royal motor-car.

he charitably dismissed them as the work of German agents. In fact, at least 80,000 men were on strike. An American who managed a rubber-tyre factory emptied his revolver into a mob that threatened to storm his premises. He was rescued by Cossacks. But what did such trivial incidents matter beside the magnificent, highly disciplined army Poincaré had seen. He lost no opportunity to speak earnestly to the Tsar. If only one could be sure what effect one's words were having on the mild little autocrat!

For the moment the anti-German party was in control in St. Petersburg, with the Tsar's uncle, the Grand Duke Nicholas Nicholaevitch, at its head. Six foot seven inches tall, bearded, slim and ramrod straight, this Romanoff enjoyed vast popularity in the army of which he was commander-in-chief. It was based, strange to say, on the brutality with which he was alleged to treat even his immediate subordinates. The Russian soldier, used to kicks and beatings, enjoyed hearing that exalted officers were similarly maltreated. The rest of the anti-German party were less impressive: Ivan Goremykin, the Prime Minister, was a worn-out old man with long whiskers who sat on a sofa reading French novels and smoking cigarettes. Maklakov, Minister of the Interior, owed his post to his ability to amuse the imperial family with his animal imitations: 'Do a panther, Nicholas Alexievitch.' Nicholas Alexievitch would then do a terrifying panther which sent Grand Duchesses into fits of laughter. As for General Sukhomlinov, the War Minister, he had lately hired a journalist to publish an interview with him, 'Russia is ready', which was widely reprinted in the Paris press. Sukhomlinov, a clever, humorous and sociable cavalryman, knew better than anyone what nonsense he was talking. The Germans were years ahead of Russia in armaments. It was doubtful, he thought, if they could ever be overtaken. But the interview helped a Stock Exchange flutter on which the Minister of War was at that moment engaged. 'It was very difficult to make Sukhomlinov work,' wrote his colleague Sazonov later, 'but to get him to speak the truth was well-nigh impossible.' Also Sukhomlinov needed money badly. He had married one extravagant woman and then another. He was perpetually in debt and in the hands of shady individuals, one of whom at least was in touch with German Intelligence. The War Minister did not inquire too closely into the background of his friends.

But there was no question of getting rid of Sukhomlinov. He amused the Tsar with his funny stories.

How much the autocrat liked to be amused! How much he hated men—like Count Witte, or Stolypin, for example—who asked him to follow complicated arguments and, by their voices, betrayed their contempt. At such moments the Tsar's pale blue eyes would glaze over; he would think of something else. And, later, his adored Alex the Tsarina would whisper in her guttural, Hessian accent, 'Be an autocrat, Nikky' and Nikky would then send a letter of dismissal to the over-bearing minister. What a relief! It was a pity indeed that he could not dismiss the whole business of the Tsardom and spend his life playing with his poor little son—or at tennis with the girls. But God—he did not doubt it—had laid this sacred burden on him and there was no escaping it. He felt himself being carried along on a stream too strong, too fast, to be resisted and at the end lay—the God who had made him Tsar alone knew what.

Nicholas II listened to the grey-faced lawyer from Lorraine who spoke with such emphasis, such assurance, about the fighting spirit of France, and her determination that she should be respected among the nations. Had he been anyone but a visiting head of state, Nikky might have found him tiresome. Poincaré was just the kind of man who, in Russia, might have received a letter of dismissal, after a particularly effusive conversation, as was the autocrat's custom. But France was Russia's friend; it was a comfort to know that she had at her head—if one could talk of the 'head' of a republic—a man of force and resolution. At the end of a talk with the Frenchman, Nikky was impressed and comforted. And how well the visitor spoke at state functions—what firmness; 'quite like an autocrat' as someone said, not in the Tsar's hearing.

·   ·   ·   ·   ·

An international crisis was at hand. The signs were multiplying.

The Austrian ambassador, Count Szapary, had returned unexpectedly to his post: 'Austria has a *coup de théâtre* in store for us,' said Poincaré, who was notably brusque with the ambassador at a reception in the Winter Palace.

On the 23rd more salutes, more anthems, and the visit was over. The President's warship set course for Stockholm.

The exact hour of departure was a matter of intense curiosity in one quarter. The Austrians went to some trouble to find out through the German Embassy when it would occur.

All over Europe people were on holiday. General von Moltke showed himself on the shady Alte Wiese at Carlsbad with his wife and daughter, a daily proof to all the world that peace was not in danger and that the German Chief of Staff did not enjoy perfect health. Admiral Tirpitz took the waters at Tarasp in Switzerland. The Kaiser was at Balholm in Norway. The kings of Bavaria and Saxony stayed in their country houses. On the surface everything seemed to have settled down after the spasm of anxiety that followed Sarajevo. But not everybody was deceived by outward appearances.

Count Benckendorff, the Russian ambassador in London, had said to his son one Wednesday early in the month: 'Cony, you had better pack and go home. I think that this time we are in for it. And I really don't know what the English will do.'

2

THE TWELVE DAYS

5

'These Pistols Go Off by Themselves'

Friday, 24 July

PRESENTING himself at six o'clock sharp at the Serbian Foreign Office, Baron Giesl, Austro-Hungarian minister in Belgrade, handed over a note from his government adding that he expected a reply in forty-eight hours. Characteristically, Pasitch, the Prime Minister of Serbia, was out of town, electioneering, and showed no desire to come back. His deputy, the Minister of Finance, made excuses. It would be difficult to arrange a Cabinet meeting in time. The Baron shrugged his shoulders, mentioned the existence of telephones and railways and held out the note to the minister, who shrank back perceptibly. 'If you won't take it,' said Giesl, 'I'll leave it on the table. Then you can do what you like with it.' The Austrian threw the envelope down and marched out. When the Serbians at last tore the envelope open and read its contents, their faces grew

59

perceptibly longer. What confronted them was one of the harshest documents in diplomatic history.

The note which Musulin, Forgach and Berchtold had concocted demanded that Serbia should formally condemn and energetically repress the 'criminal and terrorist propaganda' which had led to the Sarajevo murders. The Serbian government was to suppress all publications inciting people to hate Austria, dissolve the Narodna Obrana, prevent Serbian schools from fomenting propaganda against Austria, dismiss all officers and officials guilty of it (names to be supplied by Vienna), accept the collaboration of Austrian officials in the task of suppression, open a judicial inquiry into the murder and allow Austrian delegates to take part in it, arrest without delay two named men as accomplices, stop Serbian frontier officials from taking part in the illicit arms traffic into Bosnia, 'explain' the language of some high Serbian officials after the murder, notify Vienna without delay that all these measures had been carried out. Finally a time-limit of forty-eight hours was imposed.

Berchtold and his collaborators had produced a masterpiece.

Although a great deal of its contents were unexceptionable in the circumstances, yet the tone was rough, the time-limit peremptory and one or two of its demands could not be accepted by a Serbian government with any hope of survival—and any alternative government would certainly be more intransigent than Pasitch's. In particular, there was the insistence that Austrian officials should participate in the judicial inquiry and in suppressing the anti-Austrian propaganda in Serbia.

The appalled officials in Belgrade tried to get in touch with their evasive Prime Minister. It was not so easy. Pasitch had been making an election speech at Nish that evening, a hundred and fifty miles away. Warned by some pre-knowledge or by mere instinct of the ugly turn events were taking, he said to a companion: 'It would be a good thing to take a little rest. What do you think of going off to Salonika for two or three days incog.?' Pasitch intended to be 'out of touch' during the critical period when the ultimatum was accepted or rejected, both of them courses dangerous for him. While he waited at Nish Station for the Salonika train, word came through to the station-master's office asking him to go back to Belgrade where Baron Giesl was going to present a special kind of note. Pasitch replied 'firmly' that he would deal with the note when he returned. The train steamed in from the north, the Prime Minister's coach was coupled to it and off to Salonika and its revels went Nicholas Pasitch.

He did not go far. Thirty miles farther on, a local station-master handed him a telegram from the Crown Prince-Regent ordering him to return. Even then the fugitive Prime Minister did not turn his face homewards until he had travelled many miles more along the line that led to the south. At last, plucking up courage to return he arrived in Belgrade at five o'clock in the morning of 24 July, just two hours before the telephone rang at Paléologue's bedside in the French Embassy in St. Petersburg bringing him the news of the Austrian ultimatum.

Pasitch's first call was at the Russian Legation. 'If war is un-avoidable, we shall fight,' he said gloomily. He had reason to be dejected. The harvest was not in; it was doubtful if the peasants would obey the order to mobilize. The army was desperately short of weapons and ammunition. It had only 120,000 rifles and no heavy artillery. But the supreme question was this: *Would Russia fight in a Serbian quarrel?* Serbia would have to do what Russia told her.

At that moment the Austrian ultimatum had less than thirty-seven hours to run.

As the morning wore on, Prince von Bülow, on his morning stroll along the Unter den Linden, saw ahead of him the tall, grave figure of his successor as Chancellor, Theobald von Bethmann Hollweg. No wonder the cartoonists so often showed poor Theobald with a volume of Kant under his arm. He was a good, conscientious man, who would have done very well if he had remained a provincial official. The Prince looked with good-natured compassion on his successor, who would be sure to say something stupid about the international crisis. And here it came. 'The Tsar could not possibly give his support to regicide.'

The Prince's eyes sparkled with pleasurable anticipation. It was the perfect opening for one of his favourite stories. In 1814 the Tsar Alexander I had urged Louis XVIII to find a job for Savary. The King said that this was quite impossible as Savary had sat on the revolutionary tribunal which had sentenced Louis XVI to the guillotine. 'Is that all!' exclaimed the Tsar, 'and I who dine every day with Bennigsen and Uchacov who strangled my father!'

Bethmann Hollweg made a grimace: 'Thank God so cynical a way of looking at things belongs to the past.'

The Prince continued his stroll under the sunlit leaves, content with the effect of his story.

It had been an enjoyable day for the Kaiser on board the *Hohenzollern* anchored at Balholm. He had captivated an English clergyman with his charm and learning in a theological discussion. There was nothing he liked better. Then, after dinner, in the middle of a rowdy session of the Moselle Club, a telegram was brought. The Kaiser looked at it, flushed and put it aside until the party was over.

When the news of the ultimatum was brought to Sazonov, the Russian Foreign Minister, he exclaimed, 'It's the European war.' How near was the thought of war to the minds of Europe's diplomats! Sazonov was an impulsive man, and at that moment he was excited by the champagne, the speeches and the parades of the French state visit. He was unambitious and amiable, deeply religious and highly moral. 'He would have made an excellent candidate for the post of Procurator of the Holy Synod.' Although a Russian of the Russians, he was an Anglophile. His health was weak and his nature had a feminine strain.

By half past twelve Sazonov and the British ambassador,

Sir George Buchanan, met in Paléologue's room in the French Embassy. They were not going to find any encouragement for conciliatory or moderate counsels there. 'Be firm, be firm!' was the constant advice of the French ambassador, his spirit freshly charged by Poincaré, his mind stimulated by the thought that for four days, with the President and the Prime Minister at sea, he—Paléologue—would be in a position of unparalleled authority for an official. He would, during a critical time, be the sole available French witness to what Poincaré had said to the Russians in public and in private.

'But suppose firmness leads to war?' asked Sazonov, looking in the direction of Buchanan. Buchanan admitted that his government would want to stay neutral, which he personally was certain would be tantamount to suicide.

In Buckingham Palace Mr. Speaker Lowther, waiting to take leave of the King, sat reading about the ultimatum in the *Evening Standard*, when Sir Edward Grey was ushered in.

The British Foreign Secretary was a man of noble appearance and noble principles, a member of one of the most famous of the Liberal families of the aristocracy. Whether he possessed all the qualities needed to conduct the foreign policy of Britain at a time of latent crisis in Europe was another matter.

Just thirty years before, in Balliol College minute book, Benjamin Jowett, the Master, had written: 'Sir Edward Grey, having been repeatedly admonished for idleness and having shown himself entirely ignorant of the work set him in vacation as a condition of residence, was sent down, but allowed to come up to pass his examination in June.' It would be absurd to judge a man, after a lifetime of public service, by the rebuke to the lazy undergraduate he had once been.

Sir Edward Grey was a Foreign Secretary who distrusted the people who lived abroad. He said once: 'These foreigners must be terrible intriguers to suspect us as they do. . . . Foreign statesmen ought to receive their education at an English public school.'

That such a remark might have its comic side may not have occurred to the sincere, simple and transparently honest gentleman and old Wykehamist who, in 1914, directed the foreign policy of his country.

It would have been much better and certainly more convenient if the affairs of cantankerous Europe could all have been managed in London, at occasional meetings with the ambassadors, who, although foreigners, were men he knew and liked—Cambon, Mensdorff, Benckendorff, who in spite of his name was a Russian, and Lichnowsky, who—in spite of his name—was a German. Then there would be no crisis—and he could go down to Hampshire every week-end to fish and listen to the birds. As it was, Grey did not know many of the key figures of Europe with whom, during agonizing days, he would be locked in a desperate but muffled diplomatic struggle—Jagow, the German Foreign Minister, Berchtold, Bethmann Hollweg, Sazonov— they were comparative strangers to him. He had to guess, peering through the minds of his ambassadors, what they were thinking and what they would do. And now it was urgently necessary to guess quickly and correctly. The most remarkable fact about the British Foreign Secretary was that—apart from a non-stop journey through the Continent long ago, on his way to India, and a brief state visit to Paris in the retinue of King George V—he had never visited Europe. His was a strangely incurious mind.

Grey held in his hand the full text of the Austrian note when he met Speaker Lowther in the palace. The most formidable document ever sent by one government to another, he had said to Count Mensdorff the Austrian ambassador.

In Paris, that day, they had something more exciting to think about than diplomatic notes. Four days earlier, Mme Caillaux, second wife of a former Prime Minister, Joseph Caillaux, had appeared at the Seine Tribunal on a charge of murder. Her trial was still going on.

One afternoon in March that year she had left home and gone to Gastinne-Renette, the gunsmith's, where, with some care, rejecting a Smith and Wesson as too hard on the trigger, she had chosen a Browning. She had fired practice shots in the shooting gallery on the gunsmith's premises. After that she had loaded the pistol, put the first cartridge at the ready and driven to the offices of the *Figaro*. There she had asked for M. Gaston Calmette, the editor, and, on being shown into his room, had fired six bullets at him. She said: 'There is no justice in France. That was the only way.'

Calmette died soon afterwards.

Joseph Caillaux, husband of the murderess, was one of the most remarkable and controversial politicians of his time. The full importance of his wife's crime and her trial can be understood only in relation to what Caillaux was, what he stood for in policy and what his importance was at that moment in history.

Even in that jungle of hatred and all uncharitableness, the political world of the Third French Republic, Caillaux was hated above other men. He was hated for himself, his haughtiness, his arrogant manners, his boundless conceit. He was supposed to be partial to shady financial dealings. What is certain is that he was too tolerant of dishonesty in others. He was hated, too, for his policies. His advocacy of an income tax, in the British manner, won him the detestation of the better-off. And, worse still, Caillaux was known to believe that he could make a settlement with Germany. On what terms? At the sacrifice of what French interest, which of France's allies? These were questions which patriots asked—and answered in the most pessimistic terms.

Bald; glaring at his enemies with a hard fierce eye through his gold-rimmed eyeglass; his expression pugnacious, his voice high-pitched and querulous, Caillaux did nothing to charm his contemporaries. 'He is the most unpopular man in France,' said somebody, 'but no credit is due to him on that account.'

Not everybody hated him. He had the respect and the affection of his Radical party, the devotion of his constituency. A man of the

calibre of Adolphe Messimy, Minister of War in 1914, later a
general, wrote of Caillaux:

In thirty years of parliamentary life I have not met one man of whom I could
say as of him that he is a stranger to every preoccupation of personal egotism,
the permanent defender of the rights of the state. In a word, a veritable chief
endowed with the most eminent qualities.

This strange, acrid, untypical Frenchman was born of a well-
to-do Catholic family. His father had been minister in charge of
the Channel Tunnel project. He was a man of outstanding talent
who swiftly made his way to the highest levels of the French
administration and later to the peak of politics. He was a great
Minister of Finance.

At the time of the Agadir incident in 1911, when France and
Germany had clashed dangerously over their rights in Morocco,
Caillaux was Prime Minister. He had conducted secret negotiations with the Germans behind the back of his own Foreign
Minister and, with some well-timed support from the British
government and some spectacular selling of German funds on
the Berlin bourse in which the Russians collaborated, had brought
off what was on any reckoning a diplomatic victory. Germany
had made a noisy demonstration but in the end she had to be
content with a modest addition to her West African territories.
The victor won no laurels in his own country. A swarm of
enemies descended on him. Caillaux was accused of having
yielded to force and was driven from office.

In the early spring days of 1914 Caillaux was a source of deep
anxiety to President Poincaré. In May there would be elections;
popular sentiment was running towards the Left. It would be
difficult then to deny Caillaux the premiership. Caillaux, who in
his boundless self-confidence believed he could strike a bargain
with Germany! It would be the end of Poincaré's policy of
rigid hostility to the power beyond the Rhine, of intransigence
which only just stopped short of provocation.

Fate came to Poincaré's rescue.

A campaign of unexampled virulence against the policies,
character and private life of Caillaux broke out in the *Figaro*.

Caillaux had a remarkably thick skin. His wife Henriette had not. She was a pretty little ash blonde who had—like. Caillaux—been previously married. It distressed her to overhear a customer at the couturiers saying, 'There is the wife of that thief Caillaux.' On 10 March Gaston Calmette wrote in his newspaper the *Figaro*: 'This is the decisive instant, when it is necessary not to recoil from any procedure, however it may be condemned by our morals and our tastes.'

Henriette Caillaux knew—or thought she knew—what Calmette meant. Her husband's first wife had intercepted and kept some letters from 'Jo-jo' to 'Ri-ri', from Caillaux to Henriette, and dating from the time when the adultery had not yet been made respectable by divorce and marriage. Obviously, Calmette had secured the letters and was going to print them. Indeed, on 16 March the *Figaro* printed an intimate letter from Caillaux to his wife at the time when she was still his mistress. It was affectionate and outspoken and was signed 'Ton Jo'. When she set eyes on the hated newspaper that morning Mme Caillaux rushed to her husband, shouting hysterically, 'Are you going to let those wretches penetrate my boudoir?' Throwing the *Figaro* on the floor, she went out, slamming the door. She dismissed her cook after a bad lunch and went out to find a new one. That afternoon she killed Calmette.

Caillaux, Minister of Finance, resigned from the government at once. Until his wife was tried and acquitted there was no possibility of him challenging the foreign policy which Poincaré and his cronies directed. And there was no other challenger. Such was the political importance in that critical year of the crime of Mme Caillaux.

On the evening of Calmette's murder the Italian ambassador and his wife were giving a dinner to which M. and Mme Caillaux were invited and for which Mme Caillaux had bought a new frock that morning. Hastily the seating arrangements at the dinner-table were altered so that no gap reminded the chief guest, the President of the Republic, of an event so tragic yet, as he was bound to think, so providential. Returning to the Elysée after dinner, Poincaré found waiting for him one of his closest collaborators in the government—Louis Barthou.

Barthou was obviously in a highly emotional state. He broke out, according to a story which Poincaré later told a journalist named Gheusi: 'I have come to confess. I was behind the *Figaro* campaign. I wrote all the articles against Caillaux. I am the cause of the drama. I must punish myself. I will retire from Parliament and go into the country.' Poincaré did his best to calm Barthou down. In this, he succeeded.

It is likely, however, that Barthou was not alone in the conspiracy to bring Caillaux down. Perhaps another minister named Klotz was a party to it. And perhaps Poincaré himself knew something about it. Caillaux came to think so later on.

Nothing of this was known when the trial of Mme Caillaux opened on 20 July, the day Poincaré arrived in Russia.

It was a great social as well as judicial occasion. The drab court of the Seine Tribunal, with its dark blue walls and its seven long windows, was crowded with all Paris who had been able, by influence or bribery, to get tickets. Outside, nationalist youths, organized in the Camelots du Roi, demonstrated every day against Caillaux, who had prudently mobilized his own bodyguard of thugs.

The judges entered in a blaze of scarlet. Mme Caillaux, pale and pathetic in her simple black dress, took her place on the witness-stand. The heat in court was appalling.

The accused gave her testimony during three hours of the afternoon. 'These pistols are terrible things,' she said, with an air of bewilderment. 'They go off by themselves.' She explained that her anxiety had been lest her husband should carry out his threat and wring Calmette's neck. To prevent this ruin of a splendid political career she had gone to the newspaper office. She had intended to extort from Calmette an agreement to stop the campaign. And she had lost her head. Consider the agitation she was suffering at the time. Her father was an old-fashioned bourgeois who would have denied her his house had he known of her liaison with Caillaux before marriage. Three weeks after the day on which the *Figaro* was going to publish the letters she was due to be presented to the King and Queen of England. Above all, she was concerned about her daughter, who was at the age of marriage.

After the disappearance of the slight figure of Mme Caillaux from the witness-stand the trial lacked colour until on the fourth day Caillaux's first wife, dark and bitter, dealt scornfully with the suggestion that she had wrongly failed to destroy letters sent by Caillaux to Henriette. 'I am astonished,' she cried, 'at all the pity lavished on the intruder who wormed her way into my hearth and stole my husband.' Then she explained that she had handed over the letters to Caillaux when he had promised not to seek a divorce. Her sister had, later on, brought her photographs of two letters which she providently put in the bank. These, after a great deal of by-play in court, she handed to Caillaux's counsel.

On 24 July, when the news of the Austrian ultimatum reached the newspapers, Paris was still engrossed in the trial. Far more interesting than the complicated demands of Vienna was a tit-bit like this from a letter which Caillaux had sent to Henriette: 'I have only one consolation, to think of my little one, to see her in my arms as at Ouchy.' Overcome, Mme Caillaux fainted at this point and was carried out of court by her husband, who, throughout, treated the tribunal as if it were a room in his own house.

A red-bearded shadow of Caillaux's, named Ceccaldi, launched a vehement attack on Louis Barthou, who had been Caillaux's colleague in the government. Barthou, in reply, denied that he had given official documents to Calmette. In the course of this day's hearing it turned out the *Figaro* had not intended to print any more letters from Caillaux to his wife. The disclosure which the newspaper had promised related to an alleged attempt by Caillaux to postpone investigation of the affairs of a doubtful financier, Rochette. This document, passed to Calmette by Caillaux's enemies among his Cabinet colleagues, was the threat that the *Figaro* held over Caillaux. His wife had committed murder on a misapprehension.

The drama in the court was interrupted by a comedy on the bench. The presiding judge, who was widely believed to favour the Caillaux party, and had already been told by the first Mme Caillaux that he was afraid of her former husband, said he would adjourn the hearing. One of his colleagues said sternly, 'Sir, you dishonour us.' As the sitting ended that day there was excited talk of a duel in the Bois de Boulogne between the two justices.

On the terraces of the cafés people talked of nothing but the trial. Outside the Café Cardinal, near the *Figaro* office, the Caillaux and anti-Caillaux factions clashed furiously.

In London Winston Churchill and Lord Haldane dined with Albert Ballin, a brilliant German Jew, who, by his business genius, had made the Hamburg–Amerika Line into one of the first shipping companies in the world. Ballin asked them what Britain would do if France and Germany went to war and Germany promised not to take any French territory. The promise would not, of course, cover France's colonial possessions. Ballin got no comfort from his British friends. But he took back to Germany the firm impression that the British government was seeking to maintain peace. His last memory was of Churchill, at the moment of parting, almost with tears in his eyes as he said, 'My dear friend, don't let us go to war.' One did not need to be a Bismarck to avoid war, Ballin concluded.

In St. Petersburg sporadic rioting went on in the industrial quarter. *The Times* correspondent reported to his newspaper that six workmen had been killed by the Cossacks.

'For myself I know nothing which equals the excitement of having hooked an unexpectedly large fish on a small rod and fine tackle.'

SIR EDWARD GREY, *Fly Fishing*

6

Sir Edward at the Cottage

Saturday, 25 July

THE cottage lies on the River Itchen, five miles above Winchester. To reach it, the traveller from London, seeking solitude and peace, must plunge on foot down an avenue of limes alive (as one traveller never failed to observe) with long-tailed tits. There was no road, scarcely a path.

There the cottage came into sight, suddenly behind its sweet-briar hedge, smothered in clematis, climbing roses and honey-suckle. Beyond the house the ground sloped abruptly down to a water-meadow, to a pond where rare water-fowl could breed behind a fox-proof fence and at last to the gentle river on its way southwards from the downs to the sea. A wooden foot-bridge with a simple handrail spanned it. Standing there, a man could watch the coloured trout in the lucid water below and think about less agreeable things or, more likely, put these thoughts from his mind. It was called 'Grey's Bridge'.

It would be hard to imagine a place more placidly beautiful, more attuned to the spirit of the nature-loving man who had been coming there, week-end after week-end, for almost a quarter of a century. There he could walk, listen, see—until his sight weakened—and name the birds; refine his descriptions of nature (the 'clumsy' smell of hawthorn; 'very nearly a nasty smell'—it was exact; the man had the soul of a poet); and fish for trout in the renowned beat below the cottage.

On Saturday, 25 July 1914, Sir Edward Grey, owner of the cottage at Itchen Abbas, was, if he cared to be, the most influential statesman in Europe. He represented the one great force which did not seem to be decisively committed to one side or the other in the European confrontation: which might by a well-timed declaration of purpose swing the precarious balance of military power in one direction and induce second thoughts in the irresponsible: Britain, pacific, doubtful, hard-headed, yet full of protestations of high principle, profoundly irritating and very rich. The feelings of her people about Europe were cool: the Germans were ill-mannered and pushful—and they had won the war of 1870. The French were quarrelsome and immoral—and they had lost the war of 1870. The Russians were ignorant, numerous and mercifully far off. Nor were the British encouraged to profounder reflections by their rulers. Two days before, the Chancellor of the Exchequer, David Lloyd George, had promised the House of Commons that next year there would be a substantial economy in spending on arms. The expenditure of the last few years, he said, had been very largely for the purpose of meeting a temporary emergency. The public, glancing at advertisements in the newspapers of 'Holidays in the Harz via Harwich and the Hook', or noticing that Mrs. Asquith had given a garden party at No. 10, could see few symptoms of danger abroad or alarm at home.

Edward Grey, the man, was a moral presence in the council of Europe; capable of finding words for the ideas of right and wrong amidst the squalid commerce of politics. In the Liberal

Cabinet of Asquith there were, it is true, envious critics of Grey who, while themselves taking no steady interest in European affairs, would be quick to protest that they had not been consulted on vital questions. Asquith, Grey and Haldane had made something of a monopoly of Britain's foreign business, while other men were engrossed in social reforms or embarrassed by the antics of the women's suffragette movement, or caught up in the eternal acrimony of Irish Home Rule—a problem which seemed to be nearing flash-point and was watched closely by European strategists.

The time would come when these men would speak with some bitterness. Lloyd George, for instance, would complain of 'the suppression of vital information'. The members of the Liberal Cabinet were, in fact, amazingly willing to have their foreign policy made for them and to assume that what they did not know would probably be harmless—with the unstated proviso that, should eventual disclosure prove them wrong, they could, with a good conscience, wash their hands of the whole business. This dangerous form of hypocrisy was shared by the Foreign Secretary. Sir Edward Grey had a remarkable gift for 'veiling his mind from himself'. It is an innocent perfidy which may be as harmful as the most consummate duplicity. For example, Sir Edward was able to persuade himself and his colleagues that Britain could enter into elaborate naval and military arrangements with France while still remaining untrammelled in her right to decide when and how she would go to war. It was of a piece with the embarrassment which the Foreign Secretary felt over the rumours in Berlin newspapers about an Anglo-Russian naval agreement. That very morning Sir Edward complained to Count Benckendorff, the Russian ambassador, about this source of irritation. He felt that his reputation —almost his honour—was touched, for, using a professional economy of truth with his habitual reluctance, Grey had denied the story. He had not, however, disposed of it. The rumours had persisted. They had been repeated the night before in London by Albert Ballin when he talked to Churchill and Haldane at dinner. Grey was worried about the affair.

The truth was that naval conversations had begun at Russia's insistence. What Grey could not know was that the German government was informed about every main move in Russian policy through a spy in Benckendorff's embassy in Chesham Place. Basil von Siebert, slight-built and unassuming, a Balt of Russian nationality and German loyalty, had for six years been second secretary in the embassy. From 1912 onwards he had supplied the German Embassy with all important Russian secret despatches. In due course he passed out enough documents to make a volume of 827 pages.

Benckendorff was as mystified as Grey by the rumours in the German press. But there were, after all, a score of channels through which the secrets of Tsarist Russia could reach Berlin.

It was a busy Saturday morning for Sir Edward. Looking out through his windows at the trees, the lawns and the lake of St. James's Park, he was perhaps reminded of the cottage, the Itchen and the song of birds. The weather was dull, but 'no day in midsummer can be unrelievedly heavy if there are gold-finches in the garden and ash trees in the field beyond'.

Birds of a very different plumage came to visit him in his room. They perched in the chair on the other side of his desk, bringing no melodious song to his ears. They croaked of mobilizations and menaces. Benckendorff said that if Austria were to mobilize against Serbia the Tsar would probably put his army on a war footing. Sir Edward allowed himself the opinion that this would be a perfectly natural response. It was not a well-judged remark. Transmitted to St. Petersburg, it would in due course give encouragement to Sazonov, Russia's impulsive Foreign Minister, on a day when he needed, above all things, to be restrained.

With the German ambassador, Lichnowsky, Grey was engaged in intense negotiations at an early hour of the day, long before the sun rose.

Lichnowsky was a charming prince whose dinner parties, where the footmen wore Jan Sobieski liveries, were the talk of fashionable London. When he took up the post the Kaiser had instructed him to 'give good dinners, show yourself at the races and be *a jolly good fellow'*. Lichnowsky had done all those things. A rich, cultivated, *grand seigneur* of an aristocratic Bohemian family, Lichnowsky enjoyed the ease and grace of life in England, a taste which he shared with his buxom artistic wife. While His Serene Highness the ambassador talked amiably to Mrs. Asquith, whom he reminded of a Goya picture, the Princess reclined on her green sofa, fondling her dachshund and discussing pictures with Mr. Roger Fry, the prophet of modern art.

Lichnowsky's father, as a young man, had been compelled to leave Vienna, after a duel in which he had killed a Hungarian nobleman. He had settled in Potsdam where he had become a general in the Hussars. In Berlin it was supposed that this event had given Lichnowsky an ineradicable dislike of Austria. It was certainly true that he thought the alliance of Germany with Austria was the union of a healthy body and an invalid. Germany's natural partner in his opinion was Russia.

The ambassadors of Germany, Austria and Russia in London—Lichnowsky, Count Mensdorff and Count Benckendorff—were related to one another. This again was looked on with jealous suspicion in Berlin. In the German Foreign Office Lichnowsky was regarded as a rich impressionable dilettante, and far too liberal-minded.

There was, too, a feline side to His Serene Highness which went very well with his peevish voice, and appeared, for instance, when he wrote that the Imperial Chancellor Bethmann Hollweg, 'whose brilliant career had aroused no little amazement among his friends, was a most amiable guest and companion. It is said, too, that he played the piano rather well.' Lichnowsky was not likely to know—but it would hardly have surprised him—that in the eyes of his master in Berlin the naval attaché at his embassy was the more reliable guide to the inner meanings of British policy. Lichnowsky's role was to keep the British amused while the German fleet was being built up.

Grey had suggested to Lichnowsky—who had passed it on to Berlin—that Britain and Germany should join in asking for an extension of the time-limit on the Austrian ultimatum, and, if this failed, should press for mediation between Austria and Russia by four powers—Britain, France, Germany and Italy.

This looked like a sensible proposal. In fact it was hardly that. It suggested to the only too eager and credulous readers in the Foreign Office in Berlin that Britain was taking up a position detached alike from Austria and Russia—and was urging the French to do likewise. The Germans would be encouraged to believe that they could let the Austrians go forward because Britain at least would never intervene in a European war. If only Paul Cambon, the astute French ambassador, had still been in London that Saturday morning! He would have realized the danger. And he might have had the authority and the power of persuasion which was needed to convince Grey that he was making a mistake. But the night before, Cambon had left hurriedly for Paris, where the Quai d'Orsay, with the Foreign Minister still on the sea between St. Petersburg and Paris, was without the expert direction he could give it.

Lichnowsky sent Grey's proposal to Berlin, with his own urgent recommendation. From the earliest whisper of Austria's diplomatic action against Serbia he had been sharply critical of Berchtold. With some sarcasm he had telegraphed to von Jagow, the German Foreign Secretary: 'To brand the whole Serbian people as a nation of rascals and murderers is a somewhat difficult task.' He warned Berlin not to be misled: the British public would favour the cause of Serbia against Austria if war broke out. They would conclude that the assassination of the Archduke and his wife was being used as a mere pretext to injure an inconvenient neighbour. Jagow had retorted acidly: 'Your verdict on our policy is always appreciated by me and I am sure the Chancellor feels the same way about it. But, after all, we have an alliance with Austria, that crumbling constellation of states on the Danube.' It might not be a good investment but where else was Germany to turn? 'If we are called upon to fight we must not funk it,' said Jagow. 'But enough and too much. It is now 1 a.m. Although the arguments may not have convinced you, I know that you will give our policy your support.'

Germany was represented in London by an ambassador who expressed disapproval of his country's policy with an eloquence and force that Sir Edward Grey himself could not have surpassed.

In the Wilhelmstrasse Sir Horace Rumbold, the British Chargé d'affaires, watched distrustfully while little, smiling Jagow padded softly to and fro, or sat at his desk endlessly drawing faces of women on scraps of paper. This, after all, was a natural enough diversion in one who had recently returned from his honeymoon.

'What it amounts to,' said Rumbold, 'is that you have given Austria a blank cheque.'

Jagow gave a smile. He said that he had passed on to Count Berchtold the British proposal for mediation. This was a lie. *Jagow transmitted the message to Vienna only when he was certain that it would arrive after the expiry of the Austrian time-limit.* In a situation where the peace of the civilized world lived in a time-span counted first in days, now in hours and soon in minutes, a small unnecessary delay was imposed on the process of diplomacy. As if that process was not already cumbrous enough!

So passed—or was frittered away—the afternoon of the day on which Serbia must give her answer to the Austrian ultimatum. That answer would either resolve the crisis or produce one infinitely more alarming.

At five minutes to six, in Belgrade, Nicholas Pasitch, Prime Minister of Serbia, handed to Baron Giesl his government's reply to Austria's ultimatum. He said in his bad German: 'Part of your demands we have accepted. For the rest we place our hopes on your loyalty and chivalry as an Austrian general.' After agonized hours Serbia's doubts had been resolved by a telegram from St. Petersburg in answer to a desperate appeal from the Serbian Crown Prince. When he read it Pasitch had crossed himself: 'Good, great, gracious Tsar!'

After looking quickly through the document Pasitch had left

77

with him, Giesl saw that it was not a full acceptance of Berchtold's terms. He knew exactly what he had to do. His orders were clear and he was ready to carry them out without delay. The code-books were already burned; the luggage packed; the cars at the door of the legation. Baron Giesl, his wife and staff, arrived at Belgrade station in time to catch the 6.30 train for Austria.

At the first station beyond the Austrian frontier posts he telegraphed to Vienna and put a telephone call through to Count Tisza in Budapest. The Hungarian Prime Minister did not wait to hear what Giesl had to say. 'Did it have to be?' asked the Bible man.

At Ischl, in the charming little imperial villa, the Emperor Franz Joseph had been entertaining to luncheon the Duke and Duchess of Cumberland and the Duke and Duchess of Brunswick. It was, reports one of the other guests, 'the most mournful meal at which I have ever been present in my life. The Emperor was unrecognizable. As soon as he could do so, he rose from the table and withdrew.'

At half past five Berchtold, perhaps the most frightened man in Europe that afternoon, could stand no longer the quiet of his hotel in Ischl. White and miserable, he walked over to the Emperor's villa to wait for the telephone call from Vienna. 'At the stroke of 6 p.m. he rose as if on springs. "It is hardly likely that anything will come now. I am going out for a breath of air. If I am needed I am at my pied-à-terre at the Hotel Elizabeth." '

When the telephone bell rang in the villa Baron Margutti, the Emperor's elderly aide-de-camp, took the message to his master. The old man rose from his desk and listened to the news. 'So, after all!' he said hoarsely.

A silence followed. Then the Emperor said, 'After all, the rupture of diplomatic relations is not necessarily a *casus belli.*' Much the same consoling and delusive thought visited the mind of Count Berchtold that evening.

Sir Edward Grey set off for the country. It had been a harassing day and more—and worse—lay ahead. He was tired and oppressed in spirits. Besides, his eyesight was fading quickly. After half an hour he could barely read any more. Two months earlier, in May, the oculist had advised a six months' rest without offering him any hope of a cure. In September, when the parliamentary session was over, he would go to Germany and consult a famous specialist. In the meantime there was the cottage, the roses, the river, the trout, now at their fattest and most brilliant. And, of course, he would be in touch all the time with The Office. Even into the cottage, that refuge of peace and sanity, the snarls and menaces of Europe could penetrate, even there the ambitions and resentments of the dangerous continent would echo.

Had anyone asked Sir Edward that afternoon, 'But is there not something else you can do but *this?*' he would certainly have replied in all candour and sincerity: 'But what? But what is there to do?' And if the suggestion had been made to the careworn man, 'For instance, you could make certain that your mediation proposal really does reach Count Berchtold's eyes in time,' Sir Edward would have been amazed and grieved at such distrust of human honesty.

At Krasnoe Seloe, Serge Sazonov, the Russian Foreign Minister, announced to an extraordinary council that the Tsar had decided in principle to mobilize thirteen army corps. Four Russian military districts opposite Austria–Hungary would in that case be brought to a war footing. This was the decision but, in fact, the operation could not be carried out. It was not possible to mobilize a geographical portion of the Russian army. The Tsar did not know this. Sazonov did not know it. And the Russian Chief of Staff, General Janushkevitch, only lately appointed, had not yet found it out.

An imposing review was held on the dusty plain. The Tsar conferred commissioned rank on 2000 cadets of the St. Petersburg Military Academy. Later there was a banquet at which Baron Grunwald, the Tsar's chief equerry, found himself sitting next to his friend General Chelius, the Kaiser's personal representative in St. Petersburg.

Grunwald said, as he touched glasses with the German: 'What

79

was decided at noon I am not permitted to tell you. But it looks very serious. Let us hope we shall see each other in better times.' After this ominous little speech the two soldiers drank to each other. Then came a theatrical performance which the Grand Duke Nicholas had organized to stir up the fighting spirit of the assembled officers.

From his crimson embassy at the corner of the Troitsky Bridge, Sir George Buchanan looked across the river at the gold pencil of St. Peter and St. Paul, brilliant against the northern sky, heard the bells of the trams outside and sniffed—for the window was open—the smells of Russia. Fish oil was the chief ingredient.

Paléologue, the persistent and bombastic Frenchman, and Sazonov, at his most mercurial, had urged Britain to side with Russia and France in this crisis that was flaring up in Europe. 'You are preaching to the converted,' Buchanan had said, shrugging his shoulders. For he did not know what London would do. With a divided Cabinet in which pacifists and pro-Germans were strong and vocal—Morley, Lloyd George, Harcourt—who could be sure what would come out of the deliberations of men like those.

Seven o'clock in the evening. At the Warsaw Station, St. Petersburg, Maurice Paléologue, with the darting brown eyes that accorded so well with his grandiose, and deceptive, surname, arrived to bid farewell to his colleague Alexander Isvolski, who was leaving for Paris. The Russian diplomat's square Calmuck face above his high white collar was alive with subtlety and excitement. The scent of parma violets fought against the odours of a swirling flood of soldiers who roamed the station and stormed the trains. The two ambassadors exchanged glances.

'It's war this time,' said Isvolski, with a final embrace for the Frenchman as he climbed into the Pullman. The whistle blew. The train set off on its journey to the West.

.   .   .   .   .

In the evening, in London, Joseph Conrad, a Pole who had become first an English sailor and then an English novelist, arrived at Liverpool Street Station with his family to catch the train for Harwich. He was going to Cracow, his birthplace in Poland, by way of Hamburg.

He had passed through the city of London on his way from the quiet corner of Kent where he lived. He had not noticed anything out of the ordinary. And in the station, where an endless line of taxi-cabs arrived and departed, there seemed to be plenty of people willing to risk a trip to the Continent. After all, why not?

A month earlier, in a city in the Midlands, a friend had told him of the murder of the Archduke. It had made no particular impression: 'Can there be in the world of real men anything more shadowy than an archduke?' Asked what he thought would be the consequences of the Sarajevo murder, Conrad had answered, 'Nothing.'

Thinking like that, it seemed quite reasonable for him to set off on this family expedition to the heart of Eastern Europe, within a few hours of the expiry of the Austrian ultimatum. Waiting in Liverpool Street Station for the boat train to leave, it did not occur to Joseph Conrad that the hand of the station clock might be counting out the last hours of peace. He was hardly to be blamed. A few hours earlier Mrs. Asquith, the Prime Minister's wife, had sent her daughter Elizabeth over to Holland to stay with Mrs. George Keppel. It had been a disappointing season for the girl and Mrs. Asquith was anxious that she should have a little fun. If the cloud was not visible from 10 Downing Street how could it be seen by a novelist in Kent?

In an excited, holiday mood the Conrads left for Harwich and Hamburg. Before too many hours had passed they would see the Borkum Light. For a few days longer the beacon would continue to flash.

There was a great fluttering of imperial black and yellow flags in Vienna. The crowds in the street were more numerous than usual on a fine Saturday evening in summer. Young men dreamt of an adventurous war. Young women thought of officers and embraced them sentimentally. A pleasant fever of truculence spread among the youth of the city, infecting unlikely victims. Kokoshka, a painter, thought of buying a charger and joining the Imperial Horse Guards. One of the sons of Dr. Freud, the physician, contemplated applying for a commission in the artillery. As he saw it, it was the only chance he had, as a Jew, of visiting Russia. In another quarter of the city the young son of a Russian political émigré named Leon Trotsky got into trouble with his Austrian companions. On the walls everywhere was chalked the childish slogan, '*Alle Serben müssen sterben*'. The little Russian shouted, '*Hoch Serbien*'. He was beaten up for his pains; thus making his first acquaintance with international politics, as his father noted.

In Berlin demonstrators suddenly appeared in the streets, confident, as it were, demanding the right of way. They grew from clusters which gathered heaven only knew where into vast processions moving up the Friedrichstrasse. There were flags, drums and students in corps uniform carrying their foils. They were watched by nervous crowds lining the littered pavements. Someone had organized all this display, which the police permitted, contenting themselves with some interference with a rival pacifist procession got up by the trade unions.

The demonstration in the Freidrichstrasse had a simple theme: 'Down with Russia!'

After the blazing heat, night brought coolness and stillness to St. Petersburg. Mists seeped in from the Gulf of Finland across the marshy islands. It seemed that the rioting in the industrial area had died down. Suddenly the city was electrified by a faint, quick, pulsing murmur, which grew louder, coming from the west, and acquired as it grew attributes of sharpness, lightness, precision. After a little it could be identified: hoof-beats, the sound of a large body of horse moving at the trot. In time, it filled with its clamour the still air between the buildings of Peter's city. People went to doors and windows to look out.

They recognized the uniforms. It was the cavalry of the Guard, dragoons, cuirassiers, Cossacks, squadron after squadron, sixteen in all, riding past through the wisps of fog, hurrying back to the Tsarist capital. A thrilling and daunting spectacle.

The Grand Duke Nicholas Nicholaevitch had ordered the camp at Krasnoe Seloe to be struck. The Guards were riding into St. Petersburg to crush the rioting in the industrial quarter which German agents—and others—had fomented.

'I have been chosen to join the ranks of
Ministers who wanted to pursue a policy of
peace and had to carry on a policy of war.'
LEOPOLD COUNT BERCHTOLD

7

Designs for a Golden Bridge

Sunday, 26 July

THE Kaiser, in his yacht off Balholm, was up before six on
that Sunday morning: 'Can I go ashore for half an hour?'
he asked Admiral von Müller. Permission was granted. It was
still early morning when the Emperor returned and the *Hohenzollern* raised anchor. The ship set course and in a little while was
only a smudge of smoke on the southern horizon.

Wilhelm was hurrying back to a supreme crisis in his reign.
He was doing so without the most important of all the items of
evidence which should have been available to him. Not long after
six o'clock on the previous evening the text of the Serbian reply
to the Austrian ultimatum had been known in Vienna. Twelve
hours later it was still unknown, not only to the nerve-tormented
Ulysses off the coast of Norway but to the Foreign Office in
Berlin. Malice had taken a fresh hand in the game. Thanks to

delays in the Ballhausplatz in Vienna, the Serbian note had not reached the German Foreign Office on that Sunday, 26 July. Jagow did not set eyes on it until Monday. This was the second of a series of man-made delays which helped to turn a dangerous situation into a deadly one.

At half past nine that morning the Kaiser's younger brother, Prince Henry of Prussia, who had been yachting at Cowes, dropped in to see his cousin George at Buckingham Palace. The two royal gentlemen shook their heads in dismay over the international situation. 'The news is very bad,' said the King. 'It looks like war in Europe. You had better go back to Germany at once.' Henry said he would go down to Eastbourne to see his sister the Queen of Greece. In the evening he would return to Germany. He then put the question bluntly to cousin George, 'What will England do?'

There are two versions of the monarch's reply. The German thinks that he said, 'We shall try all we can to keep out of this and shall remain neutral.' In King George's own notes of the conversation the answer runs thus:

I don't know what we shall do. We have no quarrel with anyone and I hope we shall remain neutral. But if Germany declares war on Russia and France joins Russia, then I am afraid we shall be dragged into it. But you can be sure that I and my government will do all we can to prevent a European war.

Both George and Henry were completely honest men, even if neither was particularly clever. Each carried away a different impression of what had been said. The difference was slight but proved to be important. Henry's account—the shorter of two records neither of which was in fact complete—emphasized Britain's hope to stay neutral. George's spoke of his fear that Britain would be involved. Henry passed on his version to his brother the Kaiser as soon as he reached Germany. The news, acting on an all too emotional and unstable temperament, was to cause a traumatic experience in the Kaiser.

'Well,' said Prince Henry, at the end of the talk, 'if our two countries shall be fighting on opposite sides I trust it will not affect our own personal friendship.'

After this pious and unconvincing sentiment he shook hands with his English cousin and left. Driving down the Mall, he called at the German Embassy, where he told Prince Lichnowsky that the King was anxious that Britain and Germany, acting together with France and Italy, should keep the situation in hand. Prince Henry then drove on to Eastbourne under a cloudy summer sky.

Lichnowsky strolled over to the Foreign Office, bearer of a message from the Imperial Chancellor: Bethmann Hollweg urged Sir Edward Grey to use his influence at St. Petersburg against any form of Russian mobilization. In Berlin the air was heavy with rumours of some ill-defined and sinister activity in the Tsar's dominions. One was always prepared to believe the worst of so vast and mysterious a land.

Lichnowsky found nobody to talk to at the Foreign Office: Sir Edward was expected to return that evening: nobody knew exactly when. The ambassador decided not to carry out his instructions until next morning.

That afternoon Sir Arthur Nicolson, the diplomat at the head of the Foreign Office, a man convinced that the danger in Europe lay in Germany's aggressive appetite, came to an important decision. In the absence of his chief he sent to the powers a proposal for a conference of ambassadors in London to deal with the emergency. Two years before, this procedure had been tried, with success. Why should it not be fruitful again? There were, in fact, substantial reasons. This time one of the great powers, Austria, was engaged as a principal against Serbia, the protégé of another great power, Russia. The tension of the crisis in Europe was enormously enhanced by the brief time-limit (already exceeded) which Austria had put on its patience. Before there could be any Ambassadors' Conference in London, Austria would be required to retreat from part of the position she had taken up and agree that the rejected Serbian reply was, at any rate, sufficiently satisfactory for negotiations to begin.

What hope was there of this? Even if Berlin and Vienna had been willing to see the business transferred to London it was too much to expect that they would have consented to hand over the negotiation to that snug little trio of cousins, Benckendorff, Mensdorff and Lichnowsky, all of whom were influenced by Grey. No. An Ambassadors' Conference was too frail a craft for those seas.

Brooding over the problem in his Hampshire cottage, Sir Edward Grey had given his approval to Nicolson's initiative. He did so with no excessive confidence. But what more could be done? Over and over again, during the years that lay ahead, this question would sound in Sir Edward's ear, a reproach which could be answered but could not be silenced.

Grey's position was complex and tormenting. He had a nineteenth-century Englishman's innate conviction that Britain's role in Europe was to be its president, the convenor of its conferences—with a casting vote. Yet, as a twentieth-century statesman, aware of the changed power situation on the Continent (France so much weaker, Germany so much stronger, Austria crumbling and Russia an inchoate, incalculable mass), Grey knew that Britain was not a judge but a party in the action. It was insular but it could not be aloof. He was called upon to be an arbiter but he felt himself to be involved. He had accepted the Entente with France while pretending half to himself, and wholly to others, that it was not an alliance. He had consented to the military conversations with the French staff, shutting his eyes to the fact that they were a one-way commitment in arms—and binding in honour. Profoundly simple, honest and not a 'European', Sir Edward was driven towards equivocation and the Continent. He suffered in consequence.

The underlying duplicity which troubled him was only the reflection of a more general ambiguity in which public opinion in Britain was involved. Her high-minded people might not wish to intervene at all in a European conflict, or if they did so, only on the side of manifest, proven right. But that could not be the last word in the affair. There was Britain's security as well as

Britain's conscience to be taken into account. France might be no better than she should be in a quarrel with Germany, but as soon as the Uhlans threatened Dunkirk, Calais and Boulogne, Britain's interests would be vitally engaged. In the end foreign policy is not a moral exercise.

About the time Sir Edward Grey set off for London that Sunday evening, C. P. Scott, the Radical editor of the *Manchester Guardian*, was reading the proofs of a leading article which would appear next morning: 'We should make it plain from the first that if Russia and France go to war we shall not be in it.'

Grey knew all about Scott's attitude; he met a similar attitude every day round the Cabinet table at No. 10. He heard it from the lips of half his colleagues. How could one meet and answer such an obstinate mis-statement of the problem? Keeping Britain out of the war—that was not the issue. If there was a general war in Europe Britain must be in it—sooner or later. For better or worse. No escaping it.

Thus on Sunday, 26 July 1914, the question was: *How to prevent war from breaking out in Europe?*

Sir Edward Grey returned to London on Sunday night resolved that next morning he would put before the Cabinet the problem which Britain could no longer escape: whether or not to stand firmly beside France and Russia should war break out. The time for 'Yes' or 'No' had come. Years afterwards, wrestling with his conscience and his memories during sleepless dawns, Sir Edward recalled his own central anxiety at the time:

One danger I saw so hideous that it must be avoided and guarded against at every word. It was that France and Russia might face the ordeal of war with Germany, relying upon our support; that this support might not be forthcoming, and that we might then, when it was too late, be held responsible for having let them in for a disastrous war.

By seeing this problem thus, the Foreign Secretary had already half confessed that in his eyes the cause of peace was half lost. His mind was bent on saving the honour of Britain, on saving her associates from disaster in war. Some of his colleagues were concerned to save the peace for Britain alone; as for France and

Russia, they must look after themselves. Between those contrasted attitudes in the British Cabinet the cause of saving the peace of Europe was fumbled and lost.

The danger in which Britain stood had been lucidly seen and forcibly stated two years earlier by one of the younger members of Asquith's Cabinet who, on that Sunday evening, was hurrying back to London. Just two years before, Winston Churchill, First Lord of the Admiralty, had sent a minute to Asquith and Grey on the naval talks with the French: 'Everyone must feel who knows the facts that we have the obligation of an alliance without its advantage and, above all, without its precise definitions.'

Churchill, a battered cherub with a boyish love of combat, spent Sunday, 26 July, gaily with his children on the beach at Cromer. The telephone was not far away. At nine o'clock, and again at noon, he talked to the First Sea Lord, Prince Louis of Battenberg. Small items of information filtering into the Admiralty suggested a rising temperature. Churchill decided to return to London.

Outside the castle in Berlin the Guards band played the 'Hymn to the Austrian Kaiser' as a tribute to a bereaved and venerable monarch. In the offices of the Great General Staff, work went on at a relentless pace. General von Moltke, just back from his trying cure at Carlsbad, spent a great deal of time polishing a literary work of some importance. He was looking ahead to the day when it might be necessary for Germany to make a polite demand on the Belgian government. Moltke devoted all his skill in composition to drafting an ultimatum.

In the Wilhelmstrasse, for a few minutes, the tissue of high-minded and pompous phrases in which the nations conducted their business was torn away. Plainer terms were used.

Jules Cambon, French ambassador, was taking his leave of the German Foreign Secretary, Gottlieb von Jagow, when he paused and, with a change of voice and a direct look into the German's eyes, asked, 'Will you allow me to speak to you as man to man?' Von Jagow gave only the slightest sign of embarrassment as he nodded his consent.

'Well,' said Cambon, 'let me tell you that what you are going to undertake is stupid. You will gain nothing from it and you will risk the loss of much. France will defend herself a great deal better than you expect. And England, which committed the serious blunder of letting you crush us in 1870, will not do so again. You may be sure of that.'

'You have your information,' retorted Jagow, smiling. 'We have ours. We are sure of England's neutrality.'

He knew that Britain was absorbed in a crisis of the Irish Home Rule question which had already put a strain on the loyalty of the officer corps. He knew that the British Cabinet was split in two over its continental policy. How could a country with its leadership divided go to war?

And how could Cambon convince the Prussian that he was wrong?

The Frenchman went immediately to the British ambassador, Sir Edward Goschen, to whom he gave an account of the conversation. 'As far as my country's attitude is concerned,' said Goschen, 'I think exactly as you do. Unhappily, I am not authorized to say so.'

A Sunday conversation in St. Petersburg:

Serge Sazonov, Foreign Minister of Russia, to Count Pourtalès, Prussian junker of a half-French family, Germans ambassador: 'You must intervene in Vienna. Help us to build a golden bridge.'

Pourtalès: 'And meanwhile you will go on arming?'

Sazonov: 'Certain preparations . . . to avoid being surprised. No mobilization.'

Pourtalès: 'Such measures are extremely dangerous and may provoke counter-measures.'

Adolphe Messimy had a busy Sunday at the Ministry of War in Paris. Decisions had to be taken. Others could be postponed. He ordered the recall of officers on leave. But the conscripts were not yet brought back to their barracks. A hundred thousand of them, the tough and expert peasantry of Gaul, had been freed from military duties so that they could bring the harvest in. And for a day or two longer the work in the fields would go on.

At the end of the day the minister walked to his house along the quays that border the Seine. Sunshine fell slanting on the city and hung in golden dust above the warm streets. From the Gare D'Orsay holiday groups poured, sunburnt, noisy, joyous, their arms loaded with flowers they were bringing back from the countryside. All through his life Messimy would carry the memory of that glorious day, of the young lovers with their arms around one another, the fathers carrying sleepy children, the laughter and the sheaves of blossom.

At nine o'clock Churchill found Prince Louis waiting for him at the Admiralty with the news that he had ordered the British fleet, concentrated in the Channel, not to disperse. Churchill took this news to Sir Edward Grey, who by this time had returned to his house in Eccleston Square. Would it be helpful or the reverse to state in public what was being done with the navy? Grey was vehement for publication: it might have a steadying effect in Europe. Churchill went back to the Admiralty and, with the First Sea Lord at his elbow, drafted a communiqué.

'If the wives of statesmen start shooting
journalists, a healthy impulse may degen-
erate into an unpleasant habit.'

Anonymous French journalist

8

A Sort of Sigh

Monday, 27 July

FOR a few long seconds there was utter stillness in the Cabinet room at 10 Downing Street. Yet what Grey had just said should have come as no surprise. If anyone failed to understand how near Europe had come to the verge of disaster there was in the newspapers of that Monday morning a curt communiqué the meaning of which could hardly be doubted. It ran:

British Naval Measures
Orders to First and Second Fleets
No Manœuvre Leave.

We received the following statement from the Secretary of Admiralty at an early hour this morning:

'Orders have been given to the First Fleet, which is concentrated at Portland, not to disperse for manœuvre leave for the present. All vessels of the Second Fleet are remaining at their home ports in proximity to their balance crews.'

Speaking quietly, as one who was present remembers it, Grey

brought his colleagues sharply against an ugly and urgent duty. The time had come when the Cabinet must make up its mind whether Britain was going to take an active part with the other two powers of the Entente, or stand aside, as a neutral. Decision could no longer be deferred. Things were moving very fast. If the Cabinet was for neutrality he did not think that he was the man to carry out such a policy.

'Here he ended', writes Lord Morley, leader of the neutralist wing of the Cabinet and keeper of the conscience of Gladstonian Liberalism, 'in accents of unaffected calm and candour. The Cabinet seemed to heave a sort of sigh, and a moment or two of breathless silence fell upon us.'

It was a silence in which men made a swift and violent re-adjustment of values. Many matters were all of a sudden pushed to one side of the political counter. Men's minds were busy with forebodings, and calculations.

'I followed him', Lord Morley continues, 'expressing my intense satisfaction that he had brought the inexorable position, to which circumstance had now brought us, plainly and definitely before us. It was fairer to France and everybody else, ourselves included. . . . It was henceforth assumed that intervention meant active resort to arms.'

To arms?

About the same time an unaccountable wave of optimism was passing over Berlin. Where the cheerfulness was born it is impossible to say, but it could be breathed everywhere: in the Wilhelmstrasse, in newspaper offices, among the crowds passing under the perfumed lime trees: a lightening of the anxiety which for days had weighed upon men's hearts, and now was percept-ibly lifted wherever one went. Except on the Bourse, where prices tumbled still further. In Paris, too, a general improvement in the international situation was noted by the *Figaro*. But in London the Stock Exchange was weak. The insurance premium against war breaking out between Austria and Serbia was forty guineas per cent.

The Times published an extract from the *New York Sun*: 'A general European war would guarantee that the economic future will belong to the American continents, especially North America.'

'In the Seine Tribunal', observed the journalist Raymond Recouly, 'the atmosphere was almost one of civil war. Storm was in the air.'

All through the day the trial of Mme Caillaux moved towards its climax amidst applause in court and demonstrations outside it: cruel laughter, the exchange of contemptuous glances and all the other accompaniments of a *cause célèbre*. Every reference to the impartiality of the judges was greeted with derision. Caillaux himself, as usual, took command of the proceedings. Reading out the will of Gaston Calmette, the murdered editor of the *Figaro*, he declared that he had left £520,000, of which £320,000 had come from Mme Bourian, the mistress of M. Chauchard of the Magasins du Louvre, £80,000 had come from Chauchard himself. This left £120,000 unaccounted for. How had Calmette, son of a poor family, accumulated so much money in a few years? Caillaux, glaring round the packed court through his monocle, had no doubt of the answer. Calmette had hired his newspaper out to foreign governments. He then passed on to another and lighter topic.

Henri Bernstein, a celebrated dramatist of the period, had given evidence on behalf of the late M. Calmette. Caillaux found that Bernstein was an odd witness on matters of morality. The implication was plain to everybody in court. At the time of the Dreyfus case Bernstein, then performing his military service in the medical corps, had been repeatedly slighted by his comrades. Finally, he had deserted and fled to Belgium. In 1900, when an amnesty was granted, he returned to France, where his play *Après Moi* was produced at the Comédie Française eleven years later. The theatre was invaded by Royalist and 'patriotic' roughs armed with rattles, motor-horns and toy trumpets. A leader of the rioters declared that the authorities would have to call out the infantry, cavalry and artillery to protect the play of 'this deserter'. In fact the authorities were able to control the situation with the help of mounted police. At the end of the evening Bernstein found himself with four duels on his hands. Asked whether he would choose pistol or sword, he replied, 'Pistol *and* sword.' In one encounter he put his blade through Léon Daudet's arm.

Soon after the incident (which brought considerable free publicity to his play) Bernstein was allowed to rejoin the army, this time in the artillery (his health having improved sufficiently to enable him to serve in a combatant corps).

All this had been brought back to the memories of the crowded court by the time the Caillaux trial was adjourned for lunch. The young advocates sauntering out into the fresh air talked about their regiments, which—to judge by the news from Vienna—they would soon be rejoining.

In the corridors Bernstein, tall, broad-shouldered, dramatically pale, superbly dressed, went up to Caillaux: 'You will have news of me, M. Caillaux. It will perhaps be the first time you will have to deal with a man.' The public waited for fresh excitement.

When the hearing was resumed they were not disappointed.

From the first moment Bernstein commanded the stage. Nothing could stop him as he rushed to the witness-stand and began to pour out a torrent of words, admirably phrased, expertly inflected. While the court murmured and the judges showed their dismay, he shouted: 'Is Caillaux there? Caillaux, are you there?' As if anyone could overlook the bald figure with the monocle and the frock-coat! 'Caillaux has so little feeling that he cannot understand the love of a man for his friend.'

'This man', shouted Bernstein, 'has mounted on a coffin nailed down by his wife so as to make his voice heard.' The crowd in court cheered the dramatist and shouted their disgust for Caillaux. Fascinated, the police made no attempt to interfere. One of the judges said contemptuously, 'This is literature.' Bernstein rounded on him. 'You let Ceccaldi give evidence. I insist on giving evidence in my own way.' Then he turned to the jury: 'Gentlemen, they have read Calmette's will to you. Shameful! Gentlemen of the jury, don't be murdered by the wife of a minister. They will read out your wills.'

'Excellent!' shouted the crowd.

Bernstein dealt ironically with Mme Caillaux's counsel M. Labori: 'I pay him my homage. He said that Calmette would have asked for an acquittal. But Calmette is dead. He has four bullets in his body.'

Then, with a practised touch of pathos, the dramatist confessed the sad indiscretion of his youth: he had been young, of a low medical category. He had bitterly regretted his act of folly. 'Caillaux has said that I did not do my military service. He is a liar.'

Tumult, in which men shouted, '*À bas Caillaux!*' Bernstein shouted that he had wiped out the fault of his youth. He had enlisted. He was in the artillery. 'I have received orders to join my regiment. I leave on the fourth day of mobilization.' More tumult. 'Clear the court,' said the presiding judge, and got up, gathering his scarlet robes about him. But Bernstein had still one final shaft to deliver.

'And now,' he asked, shaking his outstretched hand at Caillaux, 'how would Caillaux behave in battle?' He paused with an expert sense of timing while the crowd waited for the answer. 'In war you have to fire the gun yourself. You do not employ a woman to do it for you!'

At this *coup de théâtre*, the fashionable public, 2000 strong in a room that would have been comfortably filled by 500, abandoned itself to passion. Men and women stood up in their seats shouting: '*Bravo, Bernstein! Hou, hou, Caillaux!*' The famous dramatist had triumphed. He left the court surrounded by enthusiastic friends.[1]

But a darker crisis than the Caillaux trial was already looming

1. Henri Bernstein lived to fight a duel at sixty-two; was deprived of his French citizenship by the Vichy government; died in Paris in 1953, aged seventy-seven.

over France, and muted the final pleas of the opposing counsel. When Maître Chenu, for the Calmette family, described how Mme Caillaux had said, on arriving at the *Figaro* office, '*Je suis la femme d'un ministre*', the accused fainted for the second time. Me. Chenu concluded on a note of lofty patriotism. There were clouds on the horizon, he said, 'but France is valiant and must rid herself of corrosive influences'. The Public Prosecutor followed, but by this time there was so much conversation in the public seats that nobody heard him ask for a verdict of guilty of wilful murder with extenuating circumstances. The jury took an hour to reach the forseeable verdict: not guilty. Caillaux crushed his wife in his arms, the crowd broke into stormy applause, led by Caillaux's hired bravos. Reporters rushed for the telephone boxes. Barristers shouted indignantly at the jury-men as they filed sheepishly out: '*A bas les vendus!* Down with those who have sold themselves!' Outside, anti-Caillaux factions launched a furious demonstration against the verdict.

In the evening there was wild excitement in the boulevards. Thousands rioted outside the *Matin* office. A crowd of Syndicalists who had been pretending to read the telegrams displayed outside the building, at the stroke of nine shouted in unison, '*A bas la guerre!*' The mounted police charged repeatedly and fighting broke out. The entrance hall of the *Figaro* office was thronged with indignant visitors who called to protest against a miscarriage of justice. The editors prepared an article for the next day which under the heading 'A Verdict of Shame', announced that 'The most enormal scandal of our epoch has just covered with mud and blood the Radical republic'. During the trial Mme Caillaux had been a pale, affecting little figure in black, apparently bowed down with the sorrows of her life. That night a reporter of the *Matin* caught sight of her, miraculously restored in spirits, in an airy little blue frock.

France turned her back upon this sinister comedy and, in one of the swiftest reversals in her history, prepared for a heroic ordeal.

But the murder of Gaston Calmette had been something more

than a macabre farce in an all-too-familiar tradition. It had kept Joseph Caillaux from public life—and probably from the premiership—during critical months. Had he been active, there would have been an end of the personal diplomacy conducted by Poincaré from the Elysée Palace. The Russians would have been discouraged from mobilizing. The British would have looked narrowly and with some suspicion at their Entente partners. And Caillaux, brilliant, arrogant, unscrupulous man of affairs, would have tried by devious negotiations to repeat his Agadir success. At least it can be said that history in that summer of 1914 would have worked itself out differently if the pistol had not gone off in Henriette Caillaux's hand on a March afternoon.

From his house in Rye, Henry James looked with mock horror on the affair: 'I cravenly avert my eyes and stop my ears—scarcely turn round even for a look at the Caillaux family. What a family, and what a trial—and what a suggestion, for *us*, of complacent self-comparisons!'

At the approach of danger, Europe began to call back her legions to the citadel.

Abel Ferry, a young politician who bore a name famous in French colonial history, was Under-Secretary of State for Foreign Affairs, with North Africa in his keeping. He cabled from Paris to General Lyautey, Resident-General in French Morocco: 'In the event of a continental war all your efforts should be directed to keeping in Morocco only the minimum of indispensable forces. The fate of Morocco will be decided in Lorraine.' In the meantime Lyautey should reduce his occupation of the country to the principal seaports.

The pro-consul in Morocco received the message without enthusiasm. It arrived at a moment when he was presiding over a meeting in Casablanca devoted to the promotion of agriculture in Morocco. 'They are completely mad!' Lyautey exploded. 'A war among Europeans is a civil war. It is the most monumental folly the world has ever committed.'

The feuds of the old continent took on a very different appearance when viewed from one of the distant outposts which Europe was thrusting forward against barbarism.

After his three weeks' cruise Wilhelm looked sunburnt and confident when he stepped off the royal train at the Wildpark Station at Potsdam and held out his hand to be kissed by his chancellor. Poor Bethmann Hollweg, what a pale and piteous mien was his as he offered his resignation to the Kaiser! It was refused. 'You have cooked this broth,' said Wilhelm unfeelingly. 'Now you are going to eat it!' And without much more delay he set off for his palace, where a day or two later he made no secret to his military companions of the opinion that Bethmann Hollweg had collapsed completely under the stress of events.

At that moment, however, on the station platform Wilhelm did not know the extent of Bethmann's failure, if failure it was and not something worse. The Chancellor had sent a telegram to catch the Kaiser on the train; in it he omitted to mention one important fact, that Grey was proposing a conference of ambassadors. This lapse can hardly have been accidental. There was a danger, of which the Chancellor was aware, that Wilhelm, without the wisdom of his officials to restrain him, might impulsively fall into this English trap and thus deprive Germany's partner, Austria, of her cheap little war in the Balkans. But since it would be necessary for Bethmann to tell the Kaiser of Grey's project when he met him at the station, a further precaution was necessary. The Chancellor sent Lichnowsky a telegram declining the British proposal. He was thus able to speak of it to the Kaiser as something which already belonged irretrievably to the past.

This was not Bethmann's only chicanery that day.

Grey had called three ambassadors to his room. To Benckendorff, the Russian, who urged that the time had come for Britain to declare herself, he had retorted, 'Churchill's orders to the First Fleet will surely be plain enough for Germany.' To Mensdorff, the Austrian, 'There is no menace in what we are doing, but owing to the possibility of a conflagration we cannot disperse our forces.' Lichnowsky, the German, had found the Foreign Secretary in a grave mood for the first time since the crisis opened. Grey had just seen the text of the Serbian note, a compliance with Austria's demands going far beyond what he had thought possible and due solely to Russian pressure on Belgrade. Would Germany now use her influence in Vienna so as to persuade Count Berchtold and his colleagues to take the Serbian reply as a basis for discussions? Germany could do so and, by doing so, would, along with Britain, save the peace of Europe. Sharing Grey's feelings to the limit, Lichnowsky sent the appeal on to Jagow. 'Our entire future relations with England', he wrote vehemently, 'depend on the success of this step of Sir Edward Grey's. . . . The British government is convinced that it lies entirely with us whether Austria shall jeopardize European peace by stubbornly pursuing a policy of prestige.'

The dilettante Prince in London was pleading with passion against the course on which his government seemed to be set. He was warning Bethmann—as far as words were capable of warning—that friendly relations between Britain and Germany would be broken if Austria were not put under restraint. But he could not take the further step which was needed to bring Bethmann to a halt. He could not say that Britain would go to war.

For on this question the actions of the British government and the words of Grey provided doubtful testimony.

Bethmann was hearing from Count Pourtalès in St. Petersburg that Russia would not fight. He was informed about the strong pacifist influences in the British Cabinet. He had a distrust, mingled with resentment, for the high-born, liberal-minded, easy-going nobleman who sat in the German Embassy in Carlton House Terrace, looking across the Mall to the trees of St. James's Park and the tower of the Foreign Office. He thought—and he was not quite wrong—that Lichnowsky had fallen under the insidious spell of Britain. Bethmann did not believe that Britain,

The End of the Race: Grand Prix de Paris, Longchamps, 28 June 1914: 'It was a boiling hot day and a wonderful race.'

The Kaiser at Balholm: 'Gifted and even brilliant; neurotic and impulsive; easily alarmed yet capable of screwing up his courage. There was a feminine streak in him that sought admiration and caressing words.'

Poincaré and the Tsar: 'How could one fail to rejoice that such magnificence and such vitality were at France's side!'

Helmuth von Moltke (below, left): 'He had read Nietzsche and Carlyle and shared his wife's interest in theosophy.'

Leopold Count Berchtold (below, right): 'Every elegance, good manners, and that is all.'

The trial of Mme Caillaux

Above—Caillaux gives evidence: 'Bald, glaring at his enemies with a hard, fierce eye.'

Below—Mme Caillaux embraces her counsel after acquittal.

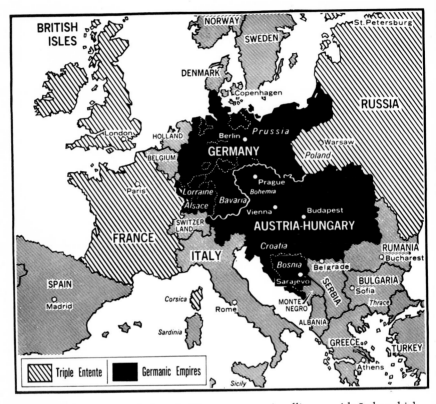

In 1914, Germany and Austria-Hungary were in alliance with Italy which, however, opted out and later intervened against them. France and Russia were allies. France had an entente with Britain, which entered the war at her side.

Serbia has since 1914 grown into Jugoslavia, by the inclusion of Montenegro, Bosnia and Croatia. Poland has been rebuilt out of territory then divided among Russia, Austria and Germany. Hungary is now separated from Austria, which has suffered the loss of the Slav areas that have become Czechoslovakia.

Alsace and Lorraine have been re-united with France.

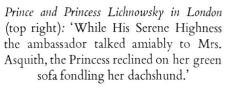

Prince and Princess Lichnowsky in London
(top right): 'While His Serene Highness
the ambassador talked amiably to Mrs.
Asquith, the Princess reclined on her green
sofa fondling her dachshund.'

*Lord Morley on his way to the Cabinet,
2 August* (right): 'A prey to deep and
melancholy reflections on men and affairs.'

Berlin, Unter den Linden, Declaration of War: 'There exist many people of this kind whose whole life is spent in hopeless monotony . . . The tocsin for general mobilization intervenes in their existence like a promise.'—Trotsky.

London, Declaration of War: 'The London public . . . was not wholly dedicated to the ideal of peace.'

Austrian vagrant in Munich: 'Adolf Hitler threw himself on his knees and thanked God to be alive at such an hour.'

French Reservists in Paris: 'Their equipment was not, however, equal to that of their enemy.'

NEUTRALITY LEAGUE ANNOUNCEMENT No. 2.

BRITONS, DO YOUR DUTY

and keep your Country out of A WICKED and STUPID WAR.

Small but powerful cliques are trying to rush you into it ; you must

DESTROY THE PLOT TO-DAY

or it will be too late.

Ask yourselves : WHY SHOULD WE GO TO WAR?

THE WAR PARTY say : We must maintain the Balance of Power, because if Germany were to annex Holland or Belgium she would be so powerful as to threaten us ; or because we are bound by treaty to fight for the neutrality of Belgium ; or because we are bound by our agreements with France to fight for her.

All these reasons are false. THE WAR PARTY DOES NOT TELL THE TRUTH

The facts are these :

1. If we took sides with Russia and France, the balance of power would be upset as it has never been before. It would make the military Russian Empire of 160,000,000 the dominant Power of Europe. You know the kind of country Russia is.

2. **We are not bound to join in a general European war to defend the neutrality of Belgium.** Our treaties expressly stipulate that our obligations under them **shall not compel us to take part in a general European war** in order to fulfil them. And if we are to fight for the neutrality of Belgium, we must be prepared to fight France as well as Germany.

3. The Prime Minister and Sir Edward Grey have both emphatically and solemnly declared in the House of Commons that we have no undertaking whatever, written or spoken, to go to war for France. We discharged our obligations in the Morocco affair. The *Entente Cordiale* was a pact of peace and not an alliance for war.

4. If Germany did attempt to annex any part of Belgium, Holland, or Normandy—and there is no reason to suppose that she would attempt such a thing—she would be weaker than she is now, for she would have to use all her forces for holding her conquests down. She would have so many difficulties like those arising out of Alsace that she would have to leave other nations alone as much as possible. But we do not know in the least that she would do these things. It would be monstrous to drag this country into war on so vague a suspicion.

It is your Duty to Save your Country from this Disaster.

ACT TO-DAY OR IT MAY BE TOO LATE

Write your member that you will try and turn him out at the next election if he does not use his influence with the Government on the side of peace.

Get your local notables to hold meetings of protest against England taking part in the war.

Make your Trade Union, your I.L.P., or B.S.P. branch pass strong resolutions.

Persuade your Clergyman or Minister to urge the need for standing clear.

Send letters to your newspapers.

There are a thousand things you can do if you really love your country.

Distribute the Leaflets of the NEUTRALITY LEAGUE.

WE WANT THOUSANDS OF HELPERS ! WRITE OR CALL AT OUR TEMPORARY OFFICES:
D. ROBERTSON, Salisbury Hotel, Salisbury Square, Fleet Street. GEORGE BENSON, 8, York Street, Manchester.

Advertisement in the 'Manchester Guardian', 4 August: 'Most of those who read and approved of its appeal were soon in soldiers' uniform.'

distracted and inclined to pacifism, would fight. Thus deluded, he could see no particular importance in the British offer of mediation. What he did next was characteristic of the pedantic, short-sighted cunning which was combined in him with a genuine strain of idealism.

That evening he sent on Grey's offer to Berchtold, advising him at the same time to reject it. All this he did without telling the Kaiser, who spent the evening in his palace at Potsdam ignorant of what his servants in Berlin were doing. To Lichnowsky, Bethmann despatched a misleading telegram which seemed to say he had begun the work of mediation in Vienna. Bethmann knew that next day Austria meant to declare war on Serbia, and in his his folly he thought that Grey would soon become reconciled to the *fait accompli*.

There was another strand in the disastrous web spun in Berlin that day. The text of the Serbian note to Austria, held up in Vienna, perhaps by design, perhaps by mere Austrian *schlamperei*, at last reached Jagow in Berlin at noon. He did not send it to Potsdam until half past nine that night, too late for the Kaiser to read it. Another morning had arrived—the morning Austria was due to declare war—before Wilhelm first set eyes on the document. Among them, clever-stupid officials in the two capitals had managed to lose the best part of two days, on a day when time was every moment more precious as the pace of the crisis quickened. 'Working to rule', the diplomats of Vienna and Berlin had produced the most expensive forty-eight hours' time-lag in the history of Europe.

Austria could not get herself into a state of war with Serbia fast enough. Yet, as a final touch of farce in the whole scrambled business, it would be impossible for the foremost Austrian patrol to cross the Serbian frontier before 12 August. This chilling information was imparted to the gay Count Berchtold by Conrad von Hötzendorff that very afternoon. There was a difference, especially in Austria, between declaring war and making it.

·   ·   ·   ·   ·

Monday, 27 July

Captain Grandclément kept the *France* at a steady eighteen to nineteen knots on her south-westerly course from the Skagerrak towards Dunkirk. The warship rolled in the heavy cross-seas so that President Poincaré's saloon shipped a good deal of salt-water. During the day a German torpedo-boat out of Cuxhaven or Emden passed the *France* and fired a salute.

At midnight, following a new and shriller cry of alarm from Lichnowsky, Bethmann telegraphed a disingenuous message to his ambassador in Vienna. It would be impossible to refuse every British suggestion for mediation: 'We should be held responsible for the conflagration by the whole world. That would also make our position impossible in our own country where we must appear to have been forced into the war.' In case Vienna should have any doubts about his meaning, Bethmann added that Berlin was 'decidedly opposed to mediation by London and only passed on the suggestion in order to satisfy England'.

'Since wars of conquest ceased, war in Europe has been declared chiefly because, in their embarrassment at having mismanaged a situation, governments did not know what else to do.'

WALTER RATHENAU, 1909

9

'Death to the Serbian Dogs'

Tuesday, 28 July

THE Kaiser rose early that morning in the vast brick New Palace which Frederick the Great had built at Potsdam during the Seven Years' War to prove to his enemies that he was not ruined. By half past seven Wilhelm was out riding in the park with General von Plessen. He had at last read the Serbian reply to Austria and in consequence he was in a buoyant mood. The note was a complete capitulation, he told Plessen. Vienna had brought off a great moral victory at the cost of a forty-eight-hour ultimatum. 'All reason for war has gone.'

What Wilhelm said to his aide-de-camp he had already scribbled in the margin of the document: 'Every reason for war drops away. Giesl might have remained quietly in Belgrade! On the strength of this, I should never have ordered mobilization!'

This sound conclusion showed that the Kaiser was paying

103

more heed to Lichnowsky's warnings than were his ministers. He was in the mood of the master who has just come back from holiday and is disposed to find that his subordinates have made a mess of things. In this case he could justly do so. Besides, he had an intuitive—if imperfect—understanding of the British temperament which was denied to men like Bethmann and Jagow.

Everything suggested to him that, since Austria had received satisfaction for her wounded *amour propre*, diplomatic action should now be taken to bring the crisis to an end. Unhappily, the full truth of the situation was not within his knowledge. He did not know that this was the day the Austrians had fixed on for their declaration of war on Serbia. He did not know that his unfaithful servants in Berlin had been holding back vital news from him so that it would arrive too late.

Unaware of the lateness of the hour, Wilhelm sat down at his desk in Potsdam and drafted a proposal for a temporary Austrian occupation of Belgrade. This was at least a sensible idea, in line with thoughts that were passing through Sir Edward Grey's head about the same time. The most sensitive element in Austria was the army, which felt that its honour had been touched by the murder of its commander-in-chief, the Archduke Franz Ferdinand. The 'Halt in Belgrade' would do much to soothe these ruffled bosoms.

At 10 a.m. the Kaiser finished drafting his instructions and, since the Potsdam telephone was never used for imperial business, sent it by hand to Bethmann.

The later history of this contribution is not without interest. Bethmann, impatiently waiting for the Austrian declaration of war which would make the Kaiser's suggestion obsolete, did nothing with it for more than twelve hours. Then he sent a telegram to Vienna which proposed not only a temporary occupation of Belgrade but also the occupation of further Serbian territory as a guarantee that there would be an integral fulfilment of Austria's demands. This telegram, so drastically altering the Kaiser's intentions, so carefully delayed in transmission, arrived in Vienna too late to be passed on to Berchtold that day. By the time it reached the Ballhausplätz it could have no influence on events.

An hour after the Kaiser had drafted his proposal Berchtold solved a small but vexatious problem of protocol which had been troubling him. How was he to declare war on Serbia? His ambassador, Giesl, had left Belgrade. He could not trust the postal service. To send a messenger under a flag of truce *before* war was declared would be without precedent and, indeed, of doubtful propriety. However, the resources of science and the Ballhausplatz were not exhausted. A telegram was sent in French via Bucharest to Belgrade:

The Royal Serbian Government not having answered in a satisfactory manner the note of July 10–23, 1914, presented by the Austro-Hungarian Minister at Belgrade, the Imperial and Royal Government are thus pledged to see to the safeguarding of their rights and interests and, with this object, to have recourse to force of arms. Austro-Hungary consequently considers herself henceforward in a state of war with Serbia. Count Berchtold, Austro-Hungarian Minister of Foreign Affairs.

Wilhelm's peace-initiative could have succeeded only if time was available and determined pressure on the Austrians was exerted. There was no time in Vienna. And there was no energy in Berlin.

In yet another capital the Austrian declaration produced an explosion of fury. Serge Sazonov knew nothing of the Kaiser's belated proposal, which in fact coincided closely with his own view that the minor points at issue between Austria and Serbia could easily be adjusted by negotiation. He knew nothing of the perfidy with which Berchtold and Bethmann had, between them, delayed the Serb reply on its way to the Kaiser. He only knew that Austria had declared war.

Sazonov obtained the Tsar's signature to two ukases of mobilization—one general, the other confined to the four military governments opposite the Austrian frontier, Moscow, Kiev, Odessa and Kazan. The two documents were placed in a portfolio and left with Janushkevitch, the Chief of Staff.

The Montenegro Parliament decided to stand by its Slav brothers of Serbia. Disgusted as he was by this precipitate action,

King Nicholas made the best of the situation. He sent a telegram to his daughter's son, Crown Prince Alexander of Serbia: 'Sweet are the sacrifices one makes for the truth and for the nation's independence. Long live my dear grandson!'

One of the younger members of Asquith's government, Herbert Samuel, entered the Cabinet room which looks over the ugly garden in Downing Street to find Sir Edward Grey sitting alone in his usual place. The German government, after pretending to fall in with the mediation plan, was now acting in a furtive and puzzling manner. The Foreign Secretary, usually so calm, broke out with a passion in his voice and an anger in his light blue eyes which Samuel never forgot: 'There's some devilry going on in Berlin!'

If 'devilry' connoted some deep and subtle malice, Grey was exaggerating. What was going forward in Berlin was a certain amount of double-dealing and more stupidity, a desire to keep the Kaiser's impetuous hands off the delicate levers of diplomacy, an excess of self-assurance among shallow-minded men, anxious to see their elaborate conspiracy through to the end.

The effect was as dangerous as devilry would have been.

When he heard the news that Berchtold had declared war the Lord Chancellor, Haldane, gave up all hope of saving peace. He thought that he recognized the forerunners of war: 'The German General Staff is in the saddle!'

After the day's work was over, Sir Edward Grey went to a musical party at Lady Glenconner's. There he heard Handel sung by Mr. Campbell MacInnes. The singer noted the 'ashen misery' in the minister's face and sent him a sympathetic note. Grey replied, a week later and from a different world, 'Handel's music will survive.'

Landing at Kiel, Prince Henry of Prussia wrote a letter to his brother the Emperor: 'I had a short talk with Georgie who said, "We shall try to keep out of this and shall remain neutral."'

The phrasing was, at best, ambiguous. But on ears waiting for a message of good cheer how sweetly it would fall!

The Russian exile Leon Trotsky was astounded by the patriotic enthusiasm of the Viennese masses. What on earth could drive Pospeszil, a working shoemaker, half German, half Czech, or Frau Maresch, the greengrocer, or the cabman Frankl, to demonstrate in the square in front of the Ministry of War? A national idea? Which? Austria–Hungary was the very negation of the idea of nationality. One had to look elsewhere for the driving force. The exile, who was of a speculative cast of mind, thought he knew where to look.

There exist many people of this kind [wrote the Russian, later on] whose whole life, day after day, is spent in hopeless monotony. It is on them that contemporary society rests. The tocsin for general mobilization breaks into their existence like a promise. Everything familiar is rejected; one enters into the kingdom of the new and the extraordinary. . . .

In the mood of the Viennese crowd which demonstrated to the glory of the Habsburg arms, I rediscovered certain traits which I had known since the October days of 1905 in Petersburg. It is not for nothing that war is often shown in history to be the mother of revolution.

Half sharing and half rejecting the emotions of those scenes in the Vienna streets, the flags, ribbons, bands, processions, the proud young soldiers in their new blue-grey uniforms, another observer looked on them with a more charitable eye, finding something majestic and even seductive in the outbreak:

A city of 2,000,000, a country of nearly 50,000,000 in that hour felt that they were participating in world history, in a moment which would never recur, and that each was called upon to cast his infinitesimal self into the glowing mass, there to be purified of all selfishness.

In the delirium, only a few housewives noticed that food prices had risen sharply in the city.

A procession joyfully sang the national anthem in the streets of Budapest.

> God bless the Magyar
> With good humour and a good harvest,
> Shield him with Thy protecting arm
> On the field of battle.

Tuesday, 28 July

Arthur Koestler, a little boy aged nine, out walking with his governess, joined the marchers, shouting, 'Death to the Serbian dogs.' He too felt the seduction of the moment.

It was a busy afternoon in St. Petersburg. Waiting in Sazonov's ante-chamber, Paléologue addressed to his German colleague Pourtalès some resounding words on the subject of peace. Pourtalès called God to witness that Germany loved peace and that history would prove her right. 'Have we really got so far that we have to invoke the judgement of history!' said Paléologue, who always allots himself the best lines to speak in his dramatized versions of history.

When Pourtalès went in to see the minister, the British ambassador, Buchanan, spoke earnestly to the Frenchman: 'I have just been begging Sazonov not to consent to any military measure which Germany could call provocative. British opinion will accept the idea of intervening in the war only if Germany is indubitably the aggressor.'

When it was his turn to see the Russian, Paléologue said urgently, 'The least imprudence on your part will lose us England's help.' Sazonov gloomily agreed. 'But our General Staff is getting restless. Even now I am having great difficulty in holding them in.'

Four days earlier the Frenchman had said to Sazonov: 'War may break out at any minute. That prospect must govern all our diplomatic action.' It was doing so already.

Unobtrusively, the needles of various barometers were moving towards 'Storm'. General von Falkenhayn, Minister of War in Berlin, ordered the German troops on manœuvres to return to barracks. All leave was stopped in the British destroyer flotillas. It was learned in London that, since Saturday, no Orient express had travelled beyond Budapest. Underwriters at Lloyds quoted a 20 per cent premium against the risk of Britain being involved in war with any continental power in the next three months.

10

To Berchtold, with Emphasis

Wednesday, 29 July

POINCARÉ arrived at the Gare du Nord at twenty minutes past one. Before disembarking from the *France* at Dunkirk he had presented the ship with an appropriate memento of his voyage, a bronze statue entitled 'Military Courage'. On the train hurrying towards Paris a first glimpse at the official reports convinced him that the situation was more serious than he had thought. This time France faced something that could not be 'arranged'. Raymond Poincaré arrived in Paris resolved that France should face it. He did not arrive unannounced or unwelcomed.

The weather was agreeable, warmer than it had been for some time, at last showing the promise of a summer that, although late, would be wonderful. But the weather was not the most remarkable aspect of the wanderer's return. Maurice Barrès, fiery

nationalist writer and apostle of the Revenge for stolen Alsace–
Lorraine, had summoned all Paris to greet the President. Barrès
himself had been at the station since half past ten to see that
everything was in readiness for an impressive display. Tricolours
were everywhere. Outside, in the approaches, thousands of
patriots stood, stern, disciplined and expectant. Poincaré was pale
and tense as he stepped from the train, the embodiment not of
war perhaps but of resolution and defiance. He was met by a great
shout of '*Vive la France*'. It followed him all the way through the
thronged, exultant streets to the Elysée. What had begun as a
polemical journalist's idea had become something deeper and
graver: after forty years of humiliation Frenchmen were speaking
to their chief of state in a tone resonant and unmistakable.

Perhaps the weather had something to do with it. A belt of
warm sunshine was moving westward, across Europe. Crowds
lingered in the streets ready to cheer and sing patriotic songs and
wave flags. Soldiers marched with an extra strut. Civilian or
military—one infected the other with a dangerous but pleasant
excitement. And the throngs, which ministers and propagandists
had worked up to this pitch of expectation, were now beginning
to send the echoes of their emotions back into the chanceries
where cool decisions became harder to take with every hour that
passed. It was so at Krasnoe Seloe, on the day of the great review;
in Vienna, where Trotsky had sought to analyse the madness;
now it had reached Paris. It would take a day or two more for
the fine weather to arrive in London.

The square-chinned lawyer from Lorraine clenched his hands
tightly; he had the greatest of trouble in preventing his emotion
from showing in his face. '*Vive la France!*'

When it was all over, stalwarts of the patriotic leagues marched
past the draped statue of Strasbourg in the Place de la Concorde.

Poincaré did not waste any time that afternoon.

According to a report by Caillaux, the President called to the
Elysée, Viviani, Isvolski and an English figure who strolled over
from his embassy in grey frock-coat and top-hat and carried his
green-lined umbrella over his shoulder as usual—Sir Francis

Bertie, the British ambassador. Poincaré put a question to his visitors: Should Russia be promised French military support if she mobilized and war then ensued?

By six o'clock, Louis Malvy, a Radical-Socialist and a violent anti-clerical, who was Viviani's Minister of the Interior, called Caillaux to his Ministry. The men were old political associates and on foreign affairs they thought much alike. When Caillaux arrived at the Ministry he found Malvy looking pale and troubled. 'Russia,' said the minister, 'has asked us if she can mobilize. We have answered, Yes. We have engaged ourselves to support her.' Caillaux's alarm gleamed through his monocle. 'Then you are exceeding the terms of the Treaty of Alliance.' Malvy shrugged his shoulders. 'But of course,' Caillaux went on, 'you have made sure of England's agreement?' Malvy replied, 'There has been no question of England.' Caillaux leaped from his chair. 'Wretch,' he shouted, 'you have unleashed the war!'

Count Pourtalès, the amiable Prussian diplomat, called twice on Sazonov during the day. In the morning he hoped that Germany's task of soothing the annoyance of the Austrians would not be made harder by a premature Russian mobilization. The Russian Foreign Minister replied that the Russian army would stand behind its frontiers, for weeks if need be. Besides, only the military districts adjoining Austria would be mobilized. When Pourtalès returned in the afternoon, the exchanges between the two men were in a sharper key. If Russia went on with her military preparations, even without a mobilization, Germany would be compelled to mobilize. And a German mobilization was synonymous with war.

'Now I see why Austria is so intransigent!' cried Sazonov.

The German rose to his feet, shouting, 'I protest with all my strength against this wounding assertion!'

'Germany,' retorted Sazonov bitterly, 'can always prove me wrong by her actions.'

The parting was stormy. There were embraces, tears and

protests. The stresses of the hour were beginning to wear down the manners and nerves of the most polished gentlemen. Bethmann was like a drowning man. The Kaiser's face was 'tragic', as Admiral Tirpitz reports. Grey's was, as we know, a mask of ashen misery.

Not long afterwards, in the same room in St. Petersburg, Sazonov was talking to the Austrian ambassador, spokesman of an empire which the Russian heartily disliked. To Szapary, Sazonov renewed the assurances he had given to Pourtalès that morning: There might be a partial Russian mobilization; a mere measure of precaution. Nothing more. After all, he pointed out, 'Austria can in any case mobilize more quickly than we can.' Then the telephone rang on the Russian minister's desk, bringing the bad news that Austrian monitors in the Danube had fired some shells into Belgrade, a deserted capital. The effect on the Russian was spectacular. He exploded: 'The Tsar is right. You are only trying to gain time by negotiating. . . . What else do you want to conquer when you are in possession of the capital? What is the use of our continuing our conversation if you act like this?'

Later Sazonov talked to the Tsar who had just received another of those messages from 'Willy' which always exerted so potent an influence on his mind. The Kaiser had begged him not to let matters drift into war. Sazonov replied that he had just heard very different music from Pourtalès. The Tsar undertook to have the discrepancy cleared up. In the meantime Sazonov was given his master's permission to discuss a general mobilization with the War Minister. Later, the Tsar agreed by telephone that the ukase mobilizing the *whole* Russian army could be issued. But just before midnight came another telegram from Willy in Potsdam: Russian military measures might compromise the Kaiser 'in my role of mediator which I have so gladly accepted on your appeal to my friendship'.

At five minutes to midnight the Tsar answered this summons. Plump and shifty Sukhomlinov, Minister of War, heard to his astonishment a voice on his telephone which plainly was that of a man unused to the instrument. The Tsar had gone downstairs to the hall in his palace where the telephone stood to countermand in person the order for a general mobilization. The War Minister protested that a cancellation was technically impossible. He transferred the Tsar to Janushkevitch, the Chief of Staff. He too said that the thing could not be done. But, formally at least, the Tsar's army was not put on a war footing that night.

In the meantime Paléologue had heard from Basily, a high official at the Russian Foreign Office, that Russia intended to mobilize thirteen army corps against Austria and would, in secret, begin to mobilize the whole of her army.

The Frenchman did not pass the news on to Paris.

The final trial of strength in Asquith's Cabinet was postponed for a little longer. But, although discussions might be inconclusive, each of the decisions that were taken edged Britain a little nearer to armed intervention if France should be attacked by Germany. Meanwhile, the lines between the opposing groups of ministers were being drawn more clearly. Lewis Harcourt, Secretary for the Colonies, son of a Victorian statesman of eminence, marshalled the forces in favour of British neutrality. Earl Beauchamp's London house in Belgrave Square became the unofficial headquarters of the movement. On the other side, the First Lord of the Admiralty, Winston Churchill, was at work 'with his best daemonic energy', organizing the interventionist party and filling it with his own combative and confident spirit. The issue was still in the balance.

After Cabinet, John Burns, the old Radical who was President of the Board of Trade, walked out on to the pavement of Downing Street with the Lord President, Lord Morley, that frail, cool, yet oddly resolute survival of another age. Pressing the old man's arm, Burns said, in his rough cockney accent: 'Now mind. We look to you to stand firm.' He meant firm for neutrality.

In the meantime, various precautions were being taken. Destroyer flotillas were called back from the Irish coast where they had been on the watch for gun-runners. Holiday leave for the London police was cancelled. In Bavaria, harvest leave for the army was called off.

At luncheon at 10 Downing Street Mrs. Asquith amazed the Archbishop of Canterbury and Lord D'Abernon by telling them that she had stopped her sister Lucy from going to France to paint and that she had telegraphed to her daughter Elizabeth to come back from Holland without delay.

When the Kaiser read his brother Henry's letter from Kiel, with its mistaken news that Georgie was resolved to stay neutral, he was quite carried away by sentimental and monarchical enthusiasm. Here was something infinitely more significant and precious than the huckstering of the politicians. The Lord's anointed was speaking to his peer over the confusion and the turmoil. 'I have the word of a king!' cried Wilhelm. 'That is sufficient for me.' He was, just then, disposed to snatch at comfort where he could find it.

Profoundly troubled by the nearness and blackness of the clouds, Grey made up his mind to speak in the plainest of language. He called Lichnowsky to the Foreign Office after lunch and made an instant impression on his visitor by the calm and gravity of his demeanour. He repeated to the Prince his suggestion that Britain, Germany, France and Italy should mediate and that Austria should—as the Kaiser had proposed a day earlier—be content to occupy Belgrade and then state her conditions. Unless some positive diplomatic action were taken there was imminent danger of a European catastrophe. As long as the conflict was confined to Russia and Austria, Britain could stand aside, but if Germany as Austria's partner and France as Russia's ally were drawn in, the situation would at once be altered. It would not be practical to stand aside for an indefinite period. 'If war breaks out,' cried Sir Edward, 'it will be the greatest catastrophe that the world has ever seen. It is far from my thoughts to wish to express any kind of threat. I only want to save you from disappointment and myself from the reproach of insincerity.'

At last, then, four days after the Austrian minister had bundled himself, his wife, his staff and his baggage out of Belgrade, the eagle at the Foreign Office had shown his claws.

The impression Grey made on Lichnowsky is apparent in every line of the cable His Serene Highness sent at once to Berlin. It arrived on Bethmann's desk a few minutes after nine o'clock that evening.

Its effect was immediate and profound on another, more exalted, personage. All down the margin of his copy of Lichnowsky's despatch, the Kaiser's emotions found vent in a splutter of angry abuse. And at the bottom he wrote:

England reveals herself in her true colours at a moment when she thinks that we are caught in the toils and, so to speak, disposed of. That common crew of shopkeepers has tried to trick us with dinners and speeches. . . . Grey proves the King a liar . . . common cur. *England alone* bears the responsibility for peace and war. . . .

In case anyone should fail to recognize the style, the imperial commentator added his initial 'W'.

Wilhelm's hysteria showed not only that he was angry but also that he was filled with alarm. For him the shock was all the more severe on account of the emotional hopes he had pinned to his brother's report of his talk with Georgie. And the Kaiser had, perhaps more acutely even than Grey, a sense of the lateness of the hour.

Mrs. Asquith went to rest before dinner earlier than usual, a prey to nervous agitation. At half past seven the Prime Minister came into the bedroom and stood quite still, his face grave. Mrs. Asquith sat up in bed and listened to what her husband had to say:

'I have sent the precautionary telegram to every part of the Empire informing all the government offices that they must prepare for war. We have been considering this for the last two years at the Committee of Imperial Defence, and it has never been done before. The last telegram was sent off at 3.30 this afternoon.'

'Has it come to this!' said Mrs. Asquith. Her husband nodded without speaking, kissed her and went out.

That night Asquith jotted down in his diary his protest against the unjust opinion which some foreigners held about Britain: 'We, the only power which has made so much as a constructive suggestion in the direction of peace, are blamed by both Russia and Germany for causing the outbreak of war!'

Walking back to his house in Carlton Gardens from Park Crescent where he had been dining with the eminent bacteriologist, Sir Almroth Wright, Arthur James Balfour, former Prime Minister, ex-leader of the Conservative party, found his mind concentrated on one exciting but uncomfortable thought. Tall, graceful and deceptively languid in appearance, he threaded the crowds of Londoners on the pavements of Regent Street, shut off from their happiness by a piece of information which he could not share with them. Earlier that day he had run into his old friend Admiral Lord Fisher in Cockspur Street. Fisher had said, with a shocking lack of discretion, 'Winston has ordered the fleet up the Channel.'

Looking at the people going happily along in the evening, Balfour said to himself that he knew war was coming to them.

Stefan Zweig, returning to Vienna in haste from a holiday on the Belgian coast, was standing in the corridor of the Orient Express when it came to a halt a mile or two over the German frontier. One goods train after another passed, going towards Belgium. The trucks were covered with tarpaulins beneath which Zweig thought he could detect the shape of guns. At the first station beyond Herbesthal he jumped down from the train to buy a newspaper. The waiting-room was locked; its windows were covered. Beyond he could hear the clank of swords and the crash of grounded rifles. Zweig remembered how indignant he had been in Ostend, how vehemently he had protested to his friends, 'You can hang me to this lamp-post if the Germans march into Belgium!'

In the offices of the Great General Staff in Berlin an important fact was noted: the German harvest was almost all gathered in. For a year to come the Fatherland could live on grain from its own fields.

After some discussion in Bethmann Hollweg's room in the Chancellery a messenger was despatched to Brussels in the evening. He carried an envelope addressed to the German minister, and containing the ultimatum over which Moltke had spent such pains three days before. The minister was not to open the envelope until Berlin gave him permission.

At half past ten Bethmann, just returned from Potsdam, asked the British ambassador to come and see him in the Wilhelm-strasse. He told Goschen that he realized Britain, in the event of war in Europe, would not allow France to be crushed. But that was not Germany's intention. Far from it! She had no territorial designs on France whatever. Goschen asked: What about the French colonies? Was Germany prepared to say that she would leave them untouched? The Chancellor could give no such promise. Unimpressed but dutiful, Goschen passed the message on to London.

He could not doubt, any more than Grey would, what was the real nature of the bargain being proposed to Britain. Germany would become the military master of Europe, her supremacy challenged by none. She could then afford to switch a greater proportion of her financial and industrial resources to the task of outbuilding Britain at sea. (For even in that desperate hour the Kaiser could not bring himself to limit the German fleet in agreement with Britain.) In the meantime, with Britain's shame-faced connivance, Germany would pocket a few of the more attractive French colonies.

But the mere fact that the proposition had been put forward showed that the German Chancellor was becoming aware of the dangers into which his policy was leading him. In fact, Bethmann Hollweg's eyes were now opened, as the Kaiser's had been in the morning, to the true, and frightening, shape of the crisis. After all, there was going to be no cheap glory for Austria in the Balkans, no lightly won diplomatic laurels for Count Berchtold. There was going to be—unless Europe could somehow be halted on its headlong, fatal course—a great war. Austria had fired the first shots; Russia was preparing and might mobilize. In that case Germany would follow suit. For it would be impossible, in the state of national feeling, for the German army to remain on a peace-time footing if the Tsar's armies were poised, ready to invade East Prussia and Galicia. On this point the ordinary Berliner thought exactly as did the hard-eyed pundits in Moltke's offices. But there was one vital difference between mobilization in Germany and elsewhere. A German mobilization was a continuous process which could not be arrested until the enemy was engaged in battle. The reason? The German plan of campaign demanded that four armies, 840,000 men, should be passed through a narrow gap, 80 miles wide, in Germany's western frontier. If these crowded armies did not keep moving forward, utter chaos would prevail. The fact was known to every staff officer in Europe. For this reason alone Germany's mobilization would be followed immediately afterwards by that of France. As for Britain—from which Lichnowsky had just transmitted the ominous words of Grey—what would she decide to do?

Bethmann could no longer assume, as he had been doing, that Britain would stay out. He was appalled at the gulf which was suddenly opening under his feet. And all because of Austria's foolhardiness, made more exasperating by Austria's shiftiness. The day before, Bethmann had written in the margin of a despatch from London:

The duplicity of Austria is intolerable. They refuse to give us information; stating expressly that Count Hoyos's statements which discussed a partition of Serbia, were a purely personal expression; at Petersburg, they are lambs with not a wicked thought in their heart, and in London their Embassy talks of giving away portions of Serbian territory to Bulgaria and Albania.

By a last-minute exorcism Bethmann sought to expel the demon which he had helped to conjure up. The demon of a war which, as General von Moltke said, would 'annihilate the civilization of Europe for decades to come'.

Theobald von Bethmann Hollweg, who played Beethoven so beautifully on the piano, who read Plato in the Greek, who was a student of Kant, sat down at his desk in the Wilhelmstrasse late at night and drafted a telegram to the ambassador in Vienna, which was sent off at five minutes to three in the morning. Its tone was more peremptory than those that had preceded it: '*Pray speak to Count Berchtold at once with great emphasis. . . .*'

So in the last hours of the 29th of July the prospect of avoiding war seemed to be more hopeful than for some time. The men who carried the heaviest burden of responsibility—Grey, the Kaiser, Bethmann Hollweg, the Tsar—had at last been moved. They saw that if nothing were done Europe would slide into a disaster which not any one of them wanted.

Grey had warned Berlin. Bethmann was drafting a cautionary note to Vienna. The Kaiser had appealed to the Tsar. And the Tsar had called off the Russian general mobilization, or thought he had done so. In Vienna Berchtold was still a victim of delusions, still believed that Austria could carry out her punitive expedition against Serbia without serious interference from Russia, which would, in any case, be held in check by the ally in shining armour in Berlin. But what Austria thought seemed just then to be a matter of minor importance. After all, it would be sixteen days before an Austrian invasion of Serbia could be launched. There should with luck be ample time to avoid a general disaster.

Sometime after midnight Adolphe Messimy had a surprise visitor at the War Ministry in the Rue St. Dominique in Paris. The minister, who was at home in bed, got up at once and hurried to his office. There, in full uniform, swaying slightly because he was very drunk (*'fort ému à la manière des officiers russes d'avant guerre'*) but deadly serious, was the burly figure of Colonel Ignatieff, Isvolski's military attaché. He brought a message from the ambassador who had just heard from St. Petersburg: The Tsar had decided to mobilize fourteen army corps opposite the Austrian frontier. The German ambassador in St. Petersburg had given warning that if these military preparations were not stopped Germany would mobilize. There was only one thing for Russia to do therefore: hasten her armaments and face the imminence of war.

Messimy at once telephoned Viviani at the Quai d'Orsay to find that Isvolski was already there with the grave news. 'Express our sincere thanks [to the French Government] for the official declaration that we can wholly rely on the help of our ally.' So ran Sazonov's telegram which Viviani read with haggard eyes and half-comprehending mind. Official declaration of help. What was Sazonov talking about? Viviani was not to know how far Paléologue had gone in pushing Russia along the path of intransigence. Nor could he grasp the truth about the 'military preparations' in Russia of which Sazonov spoke in deliberately misleading words. For Paléologue had veiled from his government the facts about the two mobilization ukases which had been signed by the Tsar and were ready to be issued. Viviani did not know that the Tsar had already issued—and withdrawn—the ukase for general mobilization. This event had happened between Sazonov sending the telegram and Viviani reading it. It was known to Paléologue, his ambassador. Convinced that he was carrying out the policy of Poincaré, Paléologue was continuing to follow an adventurous and independent course of action.

'My God!' exclaimed Viviani over the telephone to the War Minister, 'it is evident that these Russians are night birds as well as drunkards. I have just had a visit from Isvolski. Tell Ignatieff that at all costs they must avoid fireworks.'

Putting down the receiver, Messimy went back to his visitor.

He told Ignatieff that Russia should mobilize her southern army corps provided she did not inform France.

Fantastic was the house of self-deception which the rulers of Europe built for themselves: France pretended not to know that Russia was mobilizing, and delicately refrained from inquiring what might be the real meaning of Sazonov's phrase when he spoke of Russia's intention to 'hasten our armaments'. In the same way Germany had refused to ask what might be the contents of the Austrian ultimatum to Serbia, lest they be too severe and Germany share in the odium they aroused. Perhaps Sir Edward Grey could be considered a victim of the same affliction when he deluded himself that the military conversations with France brought no moral obligation upon Britain.

What Messimy put crudely to Ignatieff, Viviani phrased with more circumspection to Sazonov: acquiescing in the Russian 'precautionary and defensive measures' he hoped they would give Germany no pretext to mobilize. Could anything be more equivocal!

Viviani, a man of quick and excitable intelligence, was trying to put himself right with history and, simultaneously, was unwilling to discourage the Russians. At a moment when it was necessary to rein Russia sharply in, Viviani could not nerve himself to do so. It may be that the influence of Poincaré, that man of no doubts and no fine shades, was too strong with Viviani during those hours. The sense of failure, appearing as a sense of guilt, stayed with him (according to Aristide Briand) through the rest of his life, which ended in the asylum.

The strain of events showed itself in different ways in different places. There were seven failures on the London Stock Exchange.

When the Tsar made up his diary before going to bed, he noted: 'During the day we played tennis. The weather was magnificent. . . . I was constantly being called to the telephone.'

'The Tsar is not treacherous, but he is
weak. Weakness is not treachery, but it
fulfils all its functions.'

KAISER WILHELM II

11

'The Stone Has Started Rolling'

Thursday, 30 July

LIKE a dead whale in a golden sea, the train lay becalmed on
the East Prussian plain. Some time passed before the passengers realized that anything unusual had occurred. A day and a
half earlier they had pulled out of the station in Paris on the first
stage of their 1600-mile journey to the East. Everything had gone
as smoothly as one might expect on one of the most illustrious
of international expresses in which every conceivable luxury
pampered the important beings who used it to carry them
between the West and that gorgeous, squalid, for ever fascinating
half East, the capital of which was St. Petersburg. In Paris they
had left an atmosphere of suppressed crisis. On the way through
Germany they had seen an unusual number of soldiers on station
platforms. But that could be explained readily enough: it was the
end of the annual military training period. Now they had come

122

to a halt. The train's whistle had sounded once or twice into the empty sky. Officials had passed on the track below, talking in the loud, angry voices of their kind. And then silence, stillness, followed after a time by restlessness inside the coaches. Ladies rang for their maids, demanded tea, lemonade, explanations: 'Where are we? What is happening?'

They were a few miles from Virballen and the Russian Customs post. As for what was going on, who could say for certain? Madam could read the newspapers for herself. It seemed that the train was forbidden to go farther. Then how do we reach St. Petersburg, where we are expected, where the motor-car will be waiting at the station?

No doubt Madam can walk.

East Prussia blazed around empty and sardonic. It was a day of savage heat.

After a while, when it was obvious that the train was not going on, the passengers climbed down and discussed the ridiculous predicament. They would go forward, on foot, in a body. But what if some nervous frontier guard let off a shot? At a moment of crisis one could never tell. Someone made a suggestion which was adopted. From one of the wagons-lit a bed-sheet was brought, and tied to two walking-sticks. Behind this banner of peace and warning an army of 200 people, dressed in the height of fashion, marched to the east, along the main road which ran parallel with the railway line. They kept a sharp look-out for troops. For a time not a living soul was to be seen on the expanse of stubble fields. Then a cavalry patrol was sighted; everybody crouched in a ditch. The patrol, Uhlans, went past without paying any attention. After a bit, more cavalry—Russians this time. Princess Maria Troubetskoi led a cheer. The patrol took no notice. Two hours later the column of elegant refugees reached the huge white hall of Virballen Station. At the end of it they crossed themselves before a life-size ikon of the Saviour. Buying candles at a stall, they put them in silver holders before the painting.

The deserted Nord Express, last of its kind, remained motionless among the harvest.

Maria told the story of the adventure to her cousin, Constantine Benckendorff, when she ran into him in St. Petersburg a day or two later. By that time the world had changed.

Berchtold put off as long as possible reading the message from Berlin which the German ambassador brought. First they must lunch. Then he must change, because he was going to see the Emperor. Something in the ambassador's demeanour told Berchtold that the message from Bethmann might be tiresome. It was more agreeable to read the telegrams of congratulation which were pouring in from every part of the empire. At last, however, Berchtold knitted his brows over the phrases which Bethmann had drafted in the early hours of the morning:

'We are, of course, prepared to fulfil our duty as allies, but must decline to be dragged by Vienna wantonly into a world conflagration without having any regard paid to our counsels. Pray speak to Count Berchtold at once with great emphasis.'

It was a sensible message, over which the ghost of Bismarck might have nodded in sardonic approval. Almost thirty years earlier the Iron Chancellor had asked rhetorically, 'Are we to entangle Austria, and so Germany, in an aggressive war against Russia, a war which would at once lead to another, of defence against France?' To what could such a war lead? Victory? In that case Germany would achieve no appreciable gain 'except that the French desire for revenge might permanently be shared by the Russians'. Bethmann's telegram was followed in the course of the evening by one in the same cautionary strain, from the Kaiser to the Emperor Franz Joseph.

But, alas, the visitation of wisdom to Bethmann and his master came late and its expression lacked the trenchancy which would have brought Berchtold to his senses. But for Bethmann to write clearly meant to write frankly: to admit that the whole policy pursued up to that moment in Berlin and Vienna alike had been founded on the illusion that Britain would not fight. And that could no longer be taken for granted.

About the same time as Berchtold puzzled over the disconcerting messages from Berlin an event occurred in St. Petersburg which was destined to simplify his problem in the most thorough and disastrous manner.

At four o'clock on the afternoon of 30 July the Tsar ordered the general mobilization of the Russian army. He did so in full possession of his faculties, and after a prolonged struggle of mind and conscience. For an hour the Foreign Minister, Sazonov, had argued with him in the study at Peterhof, the windows of which open on to a view of the Gulf of Finland. The latest telegram from Willy in Potsdam had been read. It was of a disturbing nature:

> My ambassador has instructions to direct the attention of your government to the dangers and serious consequences of mobilization. Austria-Hungary has mobilized only against Serbia and only a part of their army. If Russia mobilizes against Austria-Hungary the part of mediator with which you have entrusted me in such a friendly manner, and which I have accepted at your express desire, is threatened if not rendered impossible.
> The entire weight of the decision now rests on your shoulders. You have to bear the responsibility of war or peace.

These were the words of the cousin whom the Tsar admired so much, who had so much charm and magnetism, so much brilliance, who could by turns be so dominating and so sentimental. Once, only nine years before, the two emperors had made a pact on a yacht at Björkö, in the Finnish skerries. Later on their ministers had torn it up, but it remained with each of them a sweet, if slightly embarrassing, memory. While they were signing that ill-fated document, a shaft of sunlight had shone through the cabin window and fallen on the sheet of paper. Willy had said, 'It was as though my grandfather William I and Tsar Nicholas I had clasped hands in heaven!'

With a troubled face the Tsar listened to the urgent pleas of Sazonov: 'Germany is only trying to gain time. I do not think

Your Majesty ought to hesitate any longer but issue the order for general mobilization.'

'It is a question of sending thousands and thousands of men to their deaths.'

'If Your Majesty stops our preliminary mobilization,' Sazonov replied, 'you will dislocate our military organization and disconcert our allies.' The Foreign Minister's voice went on inexorably, passionately: 'Neither Your Majesty's conscience nor mine will have anything to answer for if war breaks out. Your Majesty and your government will have done everything conceivable to spare the world this ordeal. The war will be breaking out at the hour which Germany has fixed.'

An oppressive silence fell on the room. General Tatischev, one of the entourage, broke it nervously, 'Yes, it is hard to decide.' The Tsar turned on him with an unusual irritability. 'I will decide,' he said.

Then, at the end of the long internal struggle, he spoke in a firm voice to Sazonov, 'Well, then, Sergei Dimitrievitch, telephone to the Chief of my General Staff that I give the order for general mobilization.'

The tension in the room broke. Sazonov rose, bowed and almost ran to the telephone on the floor below. He passed the order triumphantly to Janushkevitch, adding, 'Now you can smash your telephone.' This Janushkevitch had threatened to do on the previous day in order to prevent any fresh attempt to countermand the mobilization.

Through what mischance of accident, design or mere human folly, had this ominous worsening of the international crisis come about?

Sazonov was not a fool any more than the Tsar was a bloodthirsty tyrant. But he was mercurial by nature and—as he had told Pourtalès a few hours earlier—he had his full share of Slav contempt for the Austrians. The news that Austria had mobilized against Serbia, that her gunboats in the Danube had lobbed some shells into Belgrade, filled him with wild indignation. It would have been useless to point out to him at that moment that the bombardment was not only a brutal, but also a singularly futile act of war. Belgrade was a defenceless city. It was also one from which king, government and ministries had departed.

Sazonov might have sought to justify mobilization on the ground that Austria could not be allowed once again, as she had been over Bosnia in 1909, to determine events in the Balkans. A second Russian humiliation of that kind, borne with Christian resignation, would have led to Russia winning and, perhaps, earning the contempt of Europe. Her satellites would have fallen away, on seeing how she failed to answer the call for aid from one of them. And her enemies would have correspondingly exulted.

All this was in Sazonov's mind on that Thursday when the War Minister and the Chief of Staff told him that a partial mobilization in the south, against Austria alone, was impossible for technical reasons. It was all or nothing. The soldiers came to the civilian and said in effect: 'We cannot explain the difficulties of our trade. You must take it from us, however, that a third of the Tsar's army cannot be mobilized while the other two-thirds remains on a peace footing.' And the civilian, overwhelmed by ignorance of the mechanics of war, bowed to the insistence of those military men and accepted their confession of incompetence, as if it were a mere statement of the limitations set by divine ordinance upon the human mind.

Besides, Austria had declared war on Serbia. Sazonov saw that the whole of his foreign policy was at stake: the policy of the alliance with France and the Entente with Britain. If that policy were to lead only to humiliation, then . . . who could say what would happen? Count Witte, once Prime Minister of Russia, had argued publicly against the policy in the spring. He had said that for Russia wisdom lay in an accommodation with Germany. In St. Petersburg, in the very court itself, there were many important personages who shared that opinion. On the other hand, it was not likely that the anti-German party, with the Grand Duke

Nicholas at its head, would quietly accept defeat. To what desperate act these men might have been led history can only conjecture. What is certain is that a second triumph of Austrian policy in the Slav Balkans would have produced an emotional explosion in Russia. And nobody could predict what would be the limits of that upheaval.

Just at that moment, by a macabre chance, peace was deprived of one of its strangest, least reputable, allies. Rasputin, the vile hypnotic monk, the orgiast, the drunkard, had all the peasant's shrewdness as well as his animal vitality. 'Our friend', as the Tsarina called him, would surely have put in his word for caution and peace with the Empress and her husband. But 'our friend' had been stabbed in the abdomen by the knife of a jealous or disillusioned woman and lay in hospital recovering. His advice was not available.

As it chanced, too, the Tsarina was not able to devote herself to business of state. She hated the Grand Dukes, feared the war policy, distrusted the French and, although she disliked the Hohenzollerns, was herself a German. She was also a mother. Her son the Tsarevitch was a sickly haemophiliac over whom the absent Rasputin was thought to exert a soothing influence. Just on that day, in another room in Peterhof, the Tsarina nursed her boy, who was ill. When she made an attempt to influence the Tsar, Sazonov, it is said, warned her, 'You are asking the Tsar to sign his own death warrant!' Nobody should put aside as impossible any wild outcome of those feverish hours in the Tsar's palace by the sea.

Meanwhile, Berlin was a prey to the wildest rumours and excitements. At two o'clock that afternoon the *Lokalanzeiger*, a Berlin newspaper thought to be in close touch with the Kaiser's military entourage, published a special edition with the exciting and false news that Germany was mobilizing. The edition was recalled at once after 150 copies had been sold. No complete explanation has ever been given of this odd affair. Was the edition one which the newspaper kept in readiness to issue? Or was the affair a clumsy attempt to jockey the Chancellor into a course of action which he was still resisting, or to frighten the Russians into a premature mobilization, thus justifying a counter-move in Germany? If the *Lokalanzeiger* edition was intended as a snare for the Russians so that they might be provoked into some precipitate and fatal action, it was unnecessary. The Russians acted without that provocation.

But it coincided with a change in policy in the highest circles of the German army. The Kaiser had received a telegram from the Tsar announcing that military measures were coming into force which had been authorized five days before. This referred to the partial mobilization against Austria. But the Kaiser, already furious over Lichnowsky's telegram, jumped to the mistaken conclusion that the Russians were five days ahead of him. Having shrunk back from war, he now lurched towards it. He had been deceived. He must mobilize! Colonel-General von Moltke, ever anxious to please his master and friend the Kaiser, scented that the wind at Potsdam had veered once again towards adventure, and he, the sensitive leader of a military machine of smooth-flowing and implacable power, must march in step with his War Lord. Moltke prepared a telegram for his military colleague Conrad von Hötzendorff in Vienna: 'Mobilize. Germany will mobilize.'

By five o'clock in the afternoon Bethmann Hollweg confessed to the Prussian Cabinet, 'The stone has started rolling.' Rais-ing his long arms in despair at the failure of his efforts—the failure to keep the general peace, the failure to provide Austria with a comfortable little war which even she could win—he mourned to Lerchenfeld, the Bavarian minister in Berlin, 'A war nobody wants is being unleashed, as it were, by elemental forces.'

Elemental forces—that is to say, a modicum of mischief, genuine misunderstanding and, most of all, the flurry of men who were compelled to act too quickly—were at work in St. Petersburg as well as Berlin. And everywhere men opposed them too slowly and with too little energy. Grey had spoken to Lichnowsky wisely but too late. As happened again and again during those days, diplomacy was sending its fire-engines to the wrong spot: already the wind had swept the flames farther on.

The leading article in the *Manchester Guardian*, the most respected and influential Radical newspaper in Britain, was headed: 'England's Danger'. It did not lack clarity or force: 'Englishmen are not the guardians of Serbian well-being or even the peace of Europe. Their first duty is to England and the peace of England. We care as little for Belgrade as Belgrade does for Manchester. But though our neutrality ought to be assured, it is not.' Sinister forces were at work to jockey Britain into a war which was no concern of hers. Some of them worked in the open, like *The Times*; others even more treacherously in the dark.

The Fathers of the City of London called on the Chancellor of the Exchequer, David Lloyd George. Their mood, like the hour, was grave. Many City magnates were missing from the private stand at Goodwood on that cool July afternoon. There they sat, facing the Chancellor, a group of men commanding enough money to buy half a continent. Their news was black. If Britain were to go to war there would be an unprecedented financial cataclysm. They predicted a disaster from which Britain, Europe, the world, would not easily recover.

Lloyd George took them to see his Prime Minister, Asquith, whose verdict on the wise men of the City was confided to his diary that night: 'The greatest ninnies I ever had to tackle. All in a state of funk like old women chattering over teacups in a cathedral town.'

In another quarter the financiers had no better luck. Lord Rothschild asked Hugh Chisholm, financial editor of *The Times*, to change the tone of the newspaper's leading articles which were driving the country to war. Wickham Steed, political editor of the paper, commented, 'The proper answer would be a still stiffer article.'

Lord Rothschild did not confine his conciliatory efforts to Britain. He had already telegraphed an appeal to his friend the

Kaiser: 'I beg to be allowed to lay most respectfully at your feet the heart-felt prayer that Your Majesty may continue to exercise his influence in the interest of universal peace.' The venerable financier continued his entreaties until the very hour of German mobilization.

At a meeting of the Parliamentary Committee on the Ventilation of the House of Commons, members found it difficult to keep their minds on the business before them. In the afternoon two meetings of Liberal M.P.s discussed the European crisis. They heard, and heeded, a request from Grey that there should be no public statement in favour of neutrality as this might encourage a German attack on France. Mainly, though, the supporters of the government were in no belligerent mood.

Lord Kitchener of Khartoum, home on leave from his post in Egypt, passed on to two army friends he met in London an impression he had formed one day at luncheon in the German Embassy. Prince Lichnowsky had dropped a few ominous words which seemed to have only one meaning. 'If you have any friends in Germany, tell them to come home at once,' said Kitchener. 'And you can use my name in the telegram.' To the vast majority of people in Britain such pessimism would have appeared to border on madness. Europe might be on the edge of war. But this was Britain!

A correspondent in *The Times* wrote, with a touch of complacency: 'It is an undoubted benefit to the British consumer that war has been delayed until the first sheaves of the wheat crops are already in stack.' During the day the price of wheat in London rose by four shillings a quarter.

At St. Petersburg one external influence was of supreme importance—that of France. One foreigner's role was important and may have been decisive—that of France's ambassador, Maurice Paléologue.

France and Russia were bound together by a military agreement the conditions and limitations of which were plain enough:

If Germany mobilized, Russia and France must mobilize immediately without taking time to consult one another. But if Austria or Italy alone were to mobilize, then neither Russia nor France would mobilize without previous mutual agreement. These were the terms of the written but secret treaty of alliance. What was the position on the morning of 30 July? Austria had mobilized eight army corps against Serbia. Russia could not therefore mobilize on her own responsibility without restoring full freedom of action to her ally, France. Yet Sazonov took France's support for granted when urging a general mobilization on the Tsar.

A week before, Poincaré had told Paléologue in St. Petersburg: 'Austria has a *coup de théâtre* in store for us. Sazonov must be firm and we must back him up.' Poincaré was constitutional head of a republic: he had no legal power to make policy, no authority over a French ambassador. But he was a man of steely character and inflexible views. And Paléologue was his man, a willing, indeed an eager, tool of his personal policy. Paléologue could be relied on to stiffen Sazonov's resolution and reiterate the assurance of France's fidelity even beyond the terms of the treaty of alliance.

There was some doubt in Paris during 30 July what precisely was going on in St. Petersburg. Slowness of communications was partly to blame. Three hours were needed for an official telegram to be coded in St. Petersburg, sent to Paris and decoded there. But it seems that Paléologue did nothing to hasten the process.

When he heard from Sazonov, sometime in the evening, that the Tsar had given the order for general mobilization he sent the news on to Paris by the slow route through Sweden. The central telegraph office in St. Petersburg was, he explained, in such a state of confusion that he did not dare to entrust the message to it. In times of intense crisis men made strange errors of judgement but in fact the German ambassador was able to reach Berlin with a cable in an hour. And Paléologue, at the French Embassy, was only ten minutes by fast droshky from the telegraph office. It almost seems that he was not anxious for the news of the Russian general mobilization to reach Paris before the morning of the 31st, that Paléologue, ambassador of France, did not wish his government to know about Russia's grave decision in time to utter protests and warnings against it. He may have shared Sazonov's extraordinary delusion that Russia could mobilize in secret.

The extent to which Sazonov hid the truth about the mobilization, Paléologue did not tell it. Poincaré knew it and Viviani did not want to know it—this is a matter which does not now admit of exact calculation.

As the evening wore on gloom deepened in the Foreign Office in Berlin. When Theodor Wolff of the *Berliner Tageblatt* looked in he found a silence like the grave in the midst of which diplomats brooded in the old-fashioned armchairs. The old Hungarian nobleman Szogyenyi, who was the Austrian ambassador, looked like one from whom despair had drained the last drop of blood. Jagow padded in and out with a fixed, ambiguous smile.

When the mobilization release must be counter-signed in St. Petersburg, General Sukhomlinov, the Russian Minister of War, suffered from a last-minute attack of reluctance. Maklakov, Minister of the Interior, sat at a table laden with ikons and ritual lamps. He crossed himself and said, 'We cannot escape our fate.' Then he signed.

The Viennese crowds were wild for war. Bengal flares lit up the Rathaus Platz and the dome of the Burgtheater.

At a midnight meeting in Albert Ballin's house in Hamburg, a last-minute decision was taken after long discussion: the Hamburg-Amerika liner *Imperator*, pride of the German merchant fleet, would not sail next morning for New York.

At midnight George Lloyd, an active Conservative politician, saw Wickham Steed, political editor of *The Times*. 'It's all up,' he said, 'the government are going to rat.' Steed asked what the opposition leaders were going to do. Lloyd answered bitterly, 'They are going to the country to play tennis.'

The Tsar Nicholas II, Emperor and Autocrat of all the Russias, King of Poland, Grand Duke of Finland, etc., etc., made up his diary at the end of an eventful day: 'I went for a walk by myself. The weather was hot. Had a delightful bathe.'

Cassandre—*Le poète troyen est mort* . . .
La parole est au poète grec.'
JEAN GIRAUDOUX—*La Guerre de*
Troie n'aura pas Lieu

12

'One Does not kill Citizen Jaurès'

Friday, 31 July

THE day of 31 July broke fine in Berlin and promised to be hot. In the office of the General Staff, Moltke, suspicious of what was going on in St. Petersburg, reached for his telephone and asked for General Hell of the army corps at Allenstein in East Prussia.

'You at the frontier,' he said, 'do you think Russia is mobilizing?'

'I have thought so for several days,' said Hell. 'The frontier is sealed. Nobody crosses, either way. They are burning the frontier guard-houses. Red mobilization notices are said to be posted up in Mlava.'

'Get me one of those red notices,' said Moltke. Two hours later Hell had one of the posters in his possession. But by that time Moltke knew from other sources that Russia was mobilizing.

Friday, 31 July

Half an hour after talking to Hell he sent a telegram to Conrad in Vienna urging Austria to mobilize. By doing so he was overruling the advice of Bethmann and going clean against the tenor of the telegram which his own All-Highest master had sent twelve hours earlier to Franz Joseph.

In Paris that morning Mme Jaurès in her red wrapper dusted the little apartment in the Passage de la Tour with the housewifely care she had given it every morning for so many years. It was a middle-class home in Passy, a little shabby and very respectable. In the hall stood a zinc umbrella-stand. Near it hung a frock-coat the pockets of which were torn as if papers had, over a long period, been stuffed too hastily into them. In the drawing-room were family photographs in plush frames, wax flowers, a girl's fading first communion wreath. Upstairs, in the study, deal shelves loaded with books and pamphlets lined the walls. At a trestle table, a burly man, whose golden beard was streaked with grey, sat writing furiously in his shirt-sleeves. Every now and then he gulped a mouthful of coffee from a cup at his elbow.

He was the tribune of the people, Jean Jaurès, leader of the French Socialist party, founder and editor of *L'Humanité*. He was at that moment the most distinguished of all European Socialists. Apart from the political police and the initiates of small circles of exiled sectaries, few people had heard the name of Lenin.

Jaurès was a man of fifty-five, beginning to show in face and girth and an odd twitching of the right cheek the weight of years and the wear of politics. A noble spirit endowed with a grandiose innocence shone out of his blue eyes. He was the poet of crowded mass meetings held in dreary industrial suburbs. A philosopher who sought to catch in nimble, resounding sentences the vision of a better world where the workers, their lost heritage restored, would enjoy their own sense of luxury, grandeur and beauty. The virtuoso of a mellifluous, magnificent voice rumbling endlessly, persuasively, in the accent of the Midi, hypnotizing those who heard it and him who played on it. An orator with the fecund eloquence of a Lloyd George or an Aneurin Bevan, although lacking the sprightly imagery of the one or the intellectual suppleness of the other.

Through all the business of politics, journalism and oratory he had kept the provincial earnestness and childlike enthusiasm for mere knowledge which, as a brilliant young student, he had brought to Paris from the Tarn and which had enabled him, the pride of the Lycée d'Albi, to pass first into the École Normale.

Once, on a day of parliamentary tumult, Joseph Caillaux had gone to fetch Jaurès, who was due to speak. He found him immersed in a volume in the library. 'I'll be there in a few minutes,' said Jaurès. 'But do you know what I am reading? Lucian's *Symposium*!' Then he launched into an impressive extempore evocation of the pomp of imperial Rome—breaking off to go to the tribune and make a speech on a technical question. He had learnt Spanish to read *Don Quixote*, and brushed up his English so as to read Shakespeare and Hume.

This torrential orator, this revolutionary of the heart if not of the brain, had been for thirty years a fiery particle in the political firmament of France, widely loved and—by a few bitter spirits—dangerously hated. He lived, a happily married man, in suburban placidity, a model of every middle-class virtue save one; he had no sense of the importance of money. When he died it would be found that he was worth less than £400.

When he woke up at half past six on that July morning and went for his customary one hour's walk through Passy, Jean Jaurès was profoundly troubled. He was as good a Frenchman as any of his compatriots, but unlike most of them he belonged also to a sect scattered thinly over the Continent, everywhere a pitiable minority, the sect of Europeans. He had, as few men had, a sense of the precariousness of the European order, built with such frail materials after so clumsy a plan and on such dubious foundations, yet carrying so heavy and precious a load of civilization and culture.

Jaurès knew that the peace of Europe, the life of its nations, was threatened as it had not been for a century. The night before he had come back from Brussels, where at the Cirque Royal he had addressed a crowded, sweating, shouting audience of 6000 workers.

On the platform beside him there was the élite of Socialism in Europe. Rosa Luxembourg, Keir Hardie, Victor Adler, Vaillant, Vandervelde and Haase, leader of the Germans, in numbers the strongest of all the Socialist parties. Haase, a pale intellectual, told how on the previous day the Berlin workers had demonstrated against war. And there sat Rubinovitch, a Russian, who a few days before had been helping to organize the huge strike in St. Petersburg that cast a cloud over Poincaré's visit.

The gathering in Brussels was a supreme effort by the Socialist International to avert the threat that hung over the Continent.

Jaurès rose, blond and barrel-chested, bearded and benign, and a roar of affection rose from the hall. After a few minutes he could be heard as he praised the noble German Socialists who had shouted '*Nieder mit dem Kriege*' in the Unter den Linden, as he spoke of the spectre that rose every six months to affright the world. The French government worked for peace. England's government was urging wisdom on Russia. If it failed and Russia were to march tomorrow the French workman would say, 'We know no secret treaty, only the public treaty with humanity and civilization.' But there was not a moment to lose. 'Attila', he told them, 'stands at the very brink of the abyss. His horses' hoofs trample the grass of the battlefield.'

Pouring out of the hall the crowd had surged through the streets, shouting, '*À bas la guerre!*' The German minister noted the incident in his despatch to Berlin, saying only of Jaurès that he had made 'a speech the reproduction of which would be superfluous'.

At a private session of the Socialist executive, Haase, the German, said: 'The Kaiser does not want war, not out of humanity but out of cowardice. He is afraid of the consequences.'

Jaurès was not sure.

To what degree would Haase or any of his colleagues beyond the Rhine stand firm against the war party? What if they were

Germans first and Socialists afterwards? Years before, Clemenceau had said, 'Wilhelm knows he will have the whole nation at his side with the Socialists in the front rank and not one of them missing.' The uneasy sense that the Tiger might be right haunted Jaurès as the Brussels discussions dragged on.

'Work on the Austrians,' he said earnestly to Haase. It was agreed that a further anti-war meeting should be held, in Paris, in a fortnight.

Walking across the Place du Sablon with Vandervelde, the Belgian Socialist, Jaurès said, in a mood of characteristic optimism: 'It will be as it was at the time of the Agadir affair. There will be ups and downs. But things cannot fail to be arranged in the end. . . . I have two hours before my train leaves. Let's go to the museum and see your Flemish primitives again.'

When he returned to Paris that night (30 July) the first news he heard was that the Russians were mobilizing. He can hardly have doubted what that meant. With the Slav spectre before them, the German Socialists would react like every other German. He went straight to the Quai d'Orsay where he pleaded with the young under-secretary Abel Ferry that the government should put pressure on Russia to rescind or postpone the disastrous decision. He did not impress Ferry. Outside the building he caught a glimpse of one whom he had called the most dangerous man in Europe. Bitterly he said, 'That scum Isvolski is getting his war.' The Russian heard and the monocle fell from his eye.

At his usual café Jaurès read an article in *La Sociale* which said: 'If there was a chief in France who was a man, Jaurès would be put against the wall at the same time as the mobilization notices.'

That meant tomorrow in all likelihood, he thought. Or, at latest, the day after.

'We must expect to be assassinated at any street corner,' he said to a colleague from *L'Humanité*. As it was late, he went home by taxi on that evening of 30 July, profoundly dejected. But when the sun rose next morning with a promise of brilliant weather, Jaurès was himself again, capable of renewing amid doubts his faith in the everlasting sanity and goodwill of the

European workers. Perhaps, even at this hour, it would be possible to save the peace. Perhaps the German comrades would refuse to aim their rifles at their French brothers. The organized workers in every land would unite to prevent the slaughter. There would be riots, mutinies, barricades. The imbecile Tsar, the timorous Kaiser, the mad counts in Vienna, and Poincaré, that implacable man who should never have been allowed to go on his dangerous mission to Russia—all these malign forces would be smashed against the resistance of the Socialist International.

Jaurès came down from his study and buttoned his shiny old frock-coat across his powerful chest. Then he set out for the Métro station on his way to the Chamber. His step was springy. The cheerful good nature of his face lent him an air of solid vitality.

In another part of Paris a younger man had just taken an important decision. His name was Raoul Villain and he was one of those youths who are pursued by the consequences of an unhappy heredity. He was twenty-eight years of age, the son of a clerk in the Reims tribunal. His mother had been mad for twenty-six years; his father was an inordinate pursuer of women. Raoul was reserved, chaste and notably pious. In appearance he was unimpressive: fair hair, pale blue eyes, a frail beard. He affected a somewhat artistic look, suitable to one who had noble ideals, cloudy ambitions and no achievement. He had failed as a farmer, had tried school-teaching at the Lycée Stanislas and, being for the moment out of work, was living on an allowance of 125 francs a month from his father. He had come back to Paris from Reims where he had been attending the funeral of his father's mother, mad for forty years.

He was consumed by an idea which, for months, ever since one evening when he saw the *Cid* at the Comédie Française, had been taking shape in his brain. In his pocket, along with a copy of Maeterlinck's *Blue Bird*, was a revolver which he had borrowed from a friend. Raoul Villain had come to Paris for the purpose of killing Jean Jaurès.

He was a patriot who read nationalist newspapers. And the

Action Française, the chauvinist and royalist daily newspaper edited by Charles Maurras, had said only a week earlier: 'We have no wish to incite anyone to political assassination but M. Jean Jaurès may well shake in his shoes.' For a day Villain loafed around Jaurès' house in Passy. He was told, 'He is in Brussels.' On the evening of the 30th he followed four men from *L'Humanité* office to the Café du Croissant. 'Which is Jaurès?' he asked. The workman he had questioned pointed to a burly figure in a shabby frock-coat and striped trousers who seemed to be feeling the heat.

Villain decided that he had not the nerve for assassination. He retired, profoundly discouraged. The sight of an anti-war demonstration outside the office of the *Matin* added to his sense of personal failure. A Socialist newspaper had called to its readers: 'A hypnotized crowd has been surging through the boulevards crying "*Vive la guerre!*" Out then this evening at half past eight, assemble in front of the offices of the *Matin* and cry "*À bas la guerre!*" '

The response to this summons deeply affected Villain.

Next day—the 31st—at seven o'clock in the evening, the German government declared a state of *Kriegsgefahrzustand* ('danger of war'), a preliminary step to mobilization.

It came as the climax of a period of hours in which Berlin had oscillated between one line of conduct and another and had given conflicting advice to its temperamental ally in Vienna. Moltke's telegram, 'Mobilize! If you do Germany will mobilize,' was read out to Berchtold in his office. The Count thought of the opposing advice that had been given him by Bethmann and cried cynically, 'Who rules in Berlin, Moltke or Bethmann?' He decided that the soldier was the man who counted.

Before half past twelve the Austrian mobilization order was sent back from the palace, signed by His Royal and Imperial Apostolic Majesty. It was published at once.

.   .   .   .   .

'Very hideous to me', wrote Henry James to Sir Claude Phillips that night, 'is the behaviour of that forsworn old pastor of his people, the Austrian Emperor of whom, so *éprouvé* and so venerable, one had supposed better things. . . .'

By his decisive intervention in Vienna it may be said that Moltke wins his modicum of infamy in history. Yet the Chief of the German Great General Staff was not, after all, a bad man. He was, like Berchtold, a man whom destiny and an imperious master had called to a position for which he was unfitted.

Nine years earlier Count Schlieffen had retired. The glacial, corseted, monocled Chief of Staff, prophet of the attack in the West, designer and perfector of the famous 'Plan'. This strategic conception consisted of a vast wheel through Belgium by the German right wing, outflanking the French fortress line. Helmuth von Moltke had followed the man and inherited his immoral and disastrous design. He became Chief of Staff with intense reluctance and a sincere sense of his own unsuitability for the post. He was a sensitive mortal born in the stern military caste of Prussia, a man of mild aesthetic interests forced to the trade of war, an idealist in philosophy profoundly convinced that war was a means of national regeneration.

Once he had set up a studio where he copied landscapes. He had cultivated the violincello. He had read Nietzsche and Carlyle and shared his wife's interest in theosophy. In a fit of enthusiasm, following a visit to a Reinhardt production in Berlin, he had begun to translate Maeterlinck's *Pelléas et Melisande*.

Misfortune had given him the name of his uncle, the victorious Field Marshal of 1870, whose photograph stood on his desk, and chance had brought on him the favour and affection of the Kaiser, who could charm as well as order and who used the wiles of friendship as well as his divine authority as King of Prussia to persuade Moltke to become head of the German army. In his agitation the reluctant Chief of Staff had poured out his troubles to Bernhard von Bülow, then German Chancellor, while they cantered side by side round the Water Tower in the Berlin Hippodrome. An inner voice, he said, warned him that he was not the man to lead armies in war: 'I lack the power of rapid decision. I am too reflective, too conscientious. I have not the temperament that can risk all on a single throw.' At the end of this shrewd self-assessment he begged Bülow to use his influence with the Kaiser against the appointment. In vain. The Kaiser brushed aside his friend's objection: 'You can look after what work there is in peace-time; in war I am my own Chief of the General Staff.'

This was the man who, unknown to the political chiefs in Germany, sent a telegram to Vienna urging an Austrian mobilization. 'Who rules in Berlin?' asked Berchtold, 'Bethmann or Moltke?'

Five weeks later, at the crisis of the Battle of the Marne, Moltke remembered this message to Vienna. 'I am often filled with horror when I think of it', he wrote to his wife. 'As if I had to answer for this dreadful thing. Yet I could not act differently.'

The motives at work on the mind of this corpulent, neurotic Mecklenburger are not hard to guess. He was obsessed by the menace to Germany from Russia's vast population and high birth-rate. It was exactly the same fear, in different terms, as haunted the mind of French strategists when they thought of the well-filled cradles beyond the Rhine. A day would come, as Moltke knew, when the French loans would have given Russia a strategic railway network adequate to her needs. When that day came the Schlieffen Plan would have no more efficacy, for it depended upon stripping Germany's eastern frontiers of troops so as to achieve a daring concentration in the west of the great mass of the German army. Forty days after the Belgian frontier was crossed the foremost Uhlans must be within sight of the Eiffel Tower. There would then still be time to deal with the Russians—provided the Russian invasion of East Prussia was as slow as Schlieffen expected it to be, and provided the Russians had not, by stealth, gained too many days by secret mobilization.

·   ·   ·   ·   ·

As soon as he heard the news of the *Kriegsgefahrzustand*, Jaurès, like a good pupil of the École Normale, went to the library of the Chamber of Deputies and looked the word up in a German dictionary. He decided that 'state of siege' was its nearest French equivalent. Later in the day he heard through an emissary sent to France by Haase the news he had feared: *The German Socialists would obey the order to mobilize.* Already German Socialist newspapers were sounding the retreat from the anti-war position: 'Foremost in our consciousness is our duty of fighting against the tyranny of the Russian knout. Down with Tsarism!' The last hope of averting a general war in Europe through the organized opposition of the workers had crumbled. There was now only one course left to Jaurès as an honest Frenchman.

In the central hall of the Palais Bourbon he told a group of his fellow deputies that *L'Humanité* next day would publish an article of his with the heading, '*En Avant!*' 'Unhappily,' he added, 'I run the risk of being assassinated by one of those doctrinaires of pacifism who are ready for every kind of violence.'

Somebody at *L'Humanité* office reminded Jaurès that he had not eaten since morning. His colleague Longuet begged him not to go to the Café du Croissant: 'You see too many royalist thugs there. Why not the Coq d'Or?' Jaurès would not have it. There was an orchestra at the Coq d'Or. Besides, 'At the Croissant we are at home.' Going there by taxi, they narrowly escaped a collision. 'Look out, driver,' Longuet shouted in protest, 'you'll have us all killed.'

'One does not kill Citizen Jaurès,' the driver replied.

In Paris there was a run on the banks; thousands queued outside the Bank of France, which announced that it would pay no more than fifty francs of gold to depositors once a fortnight.

Suddenly the excitement reached London. Soon after ten in the morning the bell in the Stock Exchange clanged. Attendants in silk hats nailed a notice to the door: The Exchange was closed until further notice. The Bank Rate was raised from 4 per cent to 8. At Westminster the postal authorities refused to give gold in exchange for notes. It was said that £1,000,000 in gold had left London for the Continent. Insurance rates against war involving any of four powers, Britain, France, Germany and Russia, rose to sixty guineas per cent.

During that morning Sir Edward Grey, with a confused and deeply divided Cabinet behind him—a cabinet in which there was a majority against mobilization—had summoned Prince Lichnowsky to the Foreign Office. He had put Britain's position clearly before the German ambassador:

If Germany made reasonable proposals and these were rejected by France and Russia, then Britain would leave them to their fate. In any other conditions, if France were involved, Britain would inevitably be drawn in.

There was an element of bluff in all this, since nobody could be sure of the final outcome of the struggle of conscience that racked Asquith's Cabinet. In addition, it left out of account the possibility that Germany would violate the neutrality of Belgium, thus bringing into effect Britain's guarantee under a treaty of 1839.

But there was an even graver defect in Grey's statement. It came too late. Had it been made on Saturday, only six days earlier, when the British Foreign Secretary went to visit his cottage on the Itchen, then it might have been effective. But this was Friday, 31 July, and already the red mobilization notices were pasted on the walls of St. Petersburg, surprising Paléologue, who, like Sazonov, thought that Russia could mobilize in secret. Beside each red notice was a white one, informing the reservist that he would be paid a sum for his clothes, varying between five roubles and fifteen kopeks, according to value. One of the red notices had been torn down by Pourtalès, the German ambassador, who took it to Sazonov. And Sazonov had shrugged his shoulders and said that what the Tsar had decreed could not now be rescinded.

The Tsar was, about this time, strolling morosely along the

closely guarded seashore at Peterhof. 'A grey day,' he wrote in his diary, 'in keeping with my mood.'

In London, too, the sky was overcast when Grey spoke to Lichnowsky. Why had he waited so long before making so weighty a pronouncement? Later on he explained that he had to carry the Cabinet, the party, the House of Commons, and the country with him. The country was still only half aware of the nearness of the peril. The party, like the Cabinet, was divided. As for the House of Commons, it deserved the waspish contempt which the *Manchester Guardian* leader-writer directed at it. During a fateful week the appointed guardian of the national interests had not once debated the European crisis and had devoted six and a half hours to discussing the Milk and Dairies Bill. Not a word of guidance or admonition had come from Parliament on the gravest international crisis of the century.

But when Grey did at last speak out to the Germans the Cabinet conflict was still unresolved, Parliament was still divided and the public still bewildered. Grey was in no better position to commit his colleagues than he had been a week earlier.

The Austrian ultimatum to Serbia had put a match to a very short fuse. To stamp on the flame before it reached the charge was a task beyond the old-style diplomacy. Grey could not impart enough additional speed to its processes. Nor, it seems, did he realize when he spoke out to Lichnowsky that something more was required of him. He should also have spoken to Viviani, the French Prime Minister, making it clear that Britain's support for France would depend on France holding Russia back. Simultaneously, Grey should have issued a direct warning to Sazonov not to mobilize.

By the morning of 31 July that warning would have come too late. At the time Grey spoke to Lichnowsky, 'reasonable proposals' from Germany had become psychologically impossible. Russia was mobilizing. The Slav in arms stood at the gate. The Cossacks were about to flood over the ancient lands of the Teutonic Knights. Germany was in the grip of a panic which she herself had helped to promote but which was no less genuine for all that.

Berchtold, appalled by the spectre he had summoned, might consider accepting mediation with Serbia. But in Berlin the Tsar's ukase of mobilization rang the alarm bell. Bethmann Hollweg, the bewildered bureaucrat, was swept aside to make room for Moltke, the soldier with bad nerves.

That evening, down at Wargrave, Edward Goulding's house on the Thames, members of the Unionist opposition meeting in conclave heard from F. E. Smith, who had been in touch with Winston Churchill, that Asquith's Cabinet was torn in two over the problem: Should Britain go to war if Germany attacked France? There would be many resignations if the verdict was given to fight. In that event, what would be the Unionist attitude to the offer of a Coalition?

Late at night the Prime Minister drove to Buckingham Palace with Sir Walter Tyrrell of the Foreign Office. They had received a message from Berlin to say that Lichnowsky's efforts to bring about a peaceful settlement were being frustrated by the Tsar's ukase of mobilization. Exhausted as he was by a long and harrowing day, Asquith drafted an appeal for the King to send to his cousin Nikky. The King was fetched out of bed to approve the reply. 'One of my strangest experiences', wrote Asquith, 'was sitting with him, clad in a dressing-gown, while I read the message and the proposed answer.'

Meanwhile, unobtrusive preparations were made by men who could not afford to be caught unprepared because of the tormented consciences of their betters. The *London Gazette* was instructed by the Privy Council Office to keep enough staff on duty during the next three days for any work that might be needed.

The normal Europe of trade and travel was coming to a standstill. The Brussels agent of the South Eastern and Chatham

Railway telegraphed to the head office that trans-continental passengers could not travel beyond Herbesthal. The agent's news came a little late.

Chauvinist bravos roamed the streets of Paris. Warned that there might be trouble, Joseph Caillaux kept indoors. He received by telephone several threats of assassination, and at last was warned by the Prefect of Police that he must leave Paris without delay.

An intuition that the time was at hand for a settling of accounts affected millions of men, each according to his temperament.

At St. Cyr, the great military school which Napoleon founded, newly commissioned officers boisterously celebrated their promotion. One shouted, 'Let us swear that when we go into action for the first time we will wear plumes in our képis and white gloves.' Everyone within earshot took the oath. Too many kept their word.

Raoul Villain, waiting to have a haircut, read in the *Temps* about the German 'Danger of War' announcement. The barber asked why he was in such a state of emotion. About seven o'clock Villain wandered aimlessly along the boulevards. Once or twice he passed *L'Humanité* office. Then he had a good dinner in Poccardi's restaurant at a cost of seven francs, a good deal more than he usually spent on a meal. Between the pear and the cheese he wrote a note to his brother: 'I think war is inevitable. Give my most tender farewell to Papa. Buy the *Temps* of this evening. I embrace you. Letter follows. Above all, make a humble confession.'

There was only one table left at the Croissant when Jaurès and his friends arrived—a place in a corner nearest to the street. Because of the intense heat, the windows of the café were open. The curtains had been drawn to keep out the glare.

Outside *L'Humanité* office, Mme Dubois, the concierge, was

sitting on the doorstep when a fair-haired young man approached. 'Is M. Jaurès in the office?' 'Nobody at all is here,' she told him. The young man made off in the direction of the Croissant. By this time it was nearly half past nine.

About twenty to ten a journalist on the staff of the *Bonnet Rouge*, René Dolié, waved before Jaurès a coloured photograph of his little girl. 'Let me see it,' said Jaurès.

At that moment someone in the street pulled back the curtain before the open window. Someone said, 'What goes on in here?' A flash. Another. Two shots. A man's head fell forward on a table.

A woman's voice, crying: 'Jaurès is killed! They have killed Jaurès!'

A captain of the espionage service, panting and dishevelled, brought the news to the Cabinet gathered in the Elysée Palace. Exclamations of horror. An appalled silence. Louis Malvy, Minister of the Interior, entered. 'The Prefect of Police has telephoned to say that there will be a revolution in Paris in three hours. The slums will rise!'

'A foreign war and a civil war,' said one of the ministers. 'In fact, everything!'

'The Prefect of Police asks that the cavalry leaving tonight to join the covering troops should stay in Paris.'

But the Cabinet decided to hold back no more than two regiments of cuirassiers.

The rumour spread through the working-class districts that Jean Jaurès had been murdered by a Tsarist agent. The Rue de Grenelle was closed to the public so that no demonstration could reach the Russian Embassy, one wing of which was occupied by the Ochrana, the Tsarist secret police.

The body of the murdered man was carried on a stretcher through the streets, followed by an immense crowd and watched by a silent, uncertain fringe of the people of Paris. Fierce cries of *'Chapeaux bas!'* were raised by partisans. And westwards, towards the fading light, passed one who embodied, better than any other, a generation of idealism, cloudy but inflaming, a delusive hope of peace and reconciliation. The future would be colder and grimmer. The present possessed a shudder of excitement all its own.

After the Cabinet ended Viviani went at midnight to sit for a long time by the bier of the murdered man.

Raymond Recouly strolled out of the *Figaro* office an hour after midnight, having read the proofs of his article for the next day's newspaper. At the corner of the Rue Drouot and the Boulevard Montmartre he heard the deep quivering sound of a troop of cavalry. '*Ce sont les cuirassiers!*' Windows were thrown open. A fat taxi-driver hoisted himself on the roof of his cab. Led by a band of excited children, the horsemen appeared in steel and blue, as if some vision of Austerlitz had been conjured up to steady the nerves of Paris.

Attila stood on the very brink of the abyss. His horse's hoofs trampled the streets of Europe.

'Je suis leur chef, il faut que je les suive'—
CAUSSIDIÉRE
Paris prefect of police, 1848, when asked
what he was doing in an unruly mob.

13

Eleven Thousand Trains

Saturday, 1 August

IT WAS a day on which the diplomats burned their papers, paid their final calls and made, with diminishing conviction, their last efforts to save the peace of Europe which they had brought to the brink of ruin by a few days of neglect, duplicity and ill-will. In these last hours men had revulsions. When it was very late—too late—the architects of catastrophe stepped back to contemplate, in a moment of horror, what they were doing. Count Berchtold supported his elegant sang-froid with sleeping-pills. Bethmann Hollweg, with ravaged face and strained gestures, walked, a man in a nightmare. Sazonov wept and stormed. Everywhere the soldiers looked, with growing impatience and more open contempt, at the final movements of the diplomatic dance. Soon *they* would control the destiny of peoples.

But the last rites had still to be conducted.

· · · · · ·

Berlin had a glimpse of the imperial panoply of war when the Kaiser, wearing the eagle helmet and full uniform of the Cuirassiers of the Guard, drove in an open carriage from Potsdam to his palace in Berlin. The Empress sat at his side in a claret gown. Various members of the imperial family followed in other carriages. The weather was superb. Later it was announced that Crown Prince Wilhelm had been appointed commander of the First Guards Division.

At five o'clock the telephone rang in Admiral von Müller's office. It was the palace on the line. The mobilization was about to be signed; would he please come at once. Shouldering his way through the dense crowds which, seeing his uniform, cried '*Hoch!*' for the navy, Müller went to the palace where he found forkbearded Admiral Tirpitz, grim at the prospect of a war in which his navy would be relegated to a subordinate role, and Falkenhayn, spruce and handsome, a fine figure of a Prussian soldier. Moltke came in, the corpulent, sixty-six-year-old Mecklenburger who would direct the German campaign. Soon afterwards Bethmann and Jagow arrived with sensational news from London: a telegram from Lichnowsky reporting that the British government promised France would remain neutral under a British guarantee.

'That calls for champagne!' cried the Kaiser, clapping his hands with delight. Turning to the Chief of Staff he said, 'We must provisionally halt the march towards the West.'

Moltke's colour, never good, changed for the worse. At this late hour the delicate, intricate, interwoven filaments of his precious time-table of mobilization could not be altered, without some unimaginable chaos overtaking the whole exquisite schedule. Eleven thousand trains, weaving to and fro over Germany's railway system in a closely timed and sinister ballet, would in a matter of hours call into being an army of 4,000,000 well-trained, superbly equipped and tensely organized soldiers launched on a supreme design: to reach Paris in forty days! Already the trains were steaming into the sidings, the barracks were being made ready; the uniforms and the weapons were being laid out; already—General Helmuth von Moltke could hardly

speak for emotion: 'That we can't do! The whole army would
be thrown into confusion. We should lose any chance of victory.'

'Your uncle would not have given me that answer,' said the
Kaiser reproachfully. He ordered a call to be put through to
Trèves where the German advance guard was preparing to move
into neutral Luxembourg.

Losing control of himself Moltke shouted, 'If I cannot march
against France I cannot take responsibility for the war!' He stood
trembling and mottled, as if he had suffered some seizure. Tears
ran down his cheeks.

'And I,' cried Bethmann Hollweg, with equal emotion, 'can't
take responsibility for failing to examine the British note!'

Bethmann and Jagow were told to go into the aide-de-camps'
room and draft a reply to London. The Kaiser, sitting at his desk
made of wood from Nelson's *Victory*, with the text of Kipling's
'If' framed on the wall behind it, wrote out a telegram to cousin
Georgie: 'If Britain guarantees the neutrality of France I will
abandon all action against her.'

Moltke, still shaking, still distraught, telephoned to the red
brick building of the General Staff to stop the advance of the
Sixteenth Division into Luxembourg—if it could be stopped. The
general was not wholly successful. At seven o'clock, just two
hours after Müller had arrived at the palace in Berlin, half a company of German troops crossed the frontier of Luxembourg and
destroyed the telephone and telegraph equipment at the railway
station of Trois Vièrges. Half an hour later another party arrived
and ordered the first party off: there had been a mistake.

Moltke never quite got over the shock to his moral and mental
balance which was administered when the Kaiser sought to
interfere with that ultimate sanctity of the German Empire: the
mobilization plan of the army.

The woebegone figure of Count Pourtalès appeared in
Sazonov's doorway. Soon after six o'clock he called to ask if
the Russian government could give him an answer to the note

he had handed over yesterday. Sazonov replied, evasively, that while the mobilization must go on, Russia was prepared to continue negotiating. Taking a piece of paper from his pocket ('Ah,' thought Sazonov, 'the declaration of war.'), the German repeated his question. A third time and with mounting emotion, Pourtalès put the question. '*Je n'ai pas d'autre réponse à vous donner*,' said the Russian. Pourtalès then, with shaking hand, passed over the declaration of war and burst into tears.

Baron von Schoen, wearing a soft black felt hat, and looking quite worn out with worry, called to see M. Viviani in his crimson and gold room at the Quai d'Orsay. He asked what France would do. If France would stay neutral, then the Baron was to ask that the fortresses of Toul and Verdun should be handed over as a pledge of good behaviour. Schoen lacked the effrontery to put forward this shameless demand—of which the French government was in any case aware, through deciphering German telegrams. Viviani said simply, 'France will have regard to her interests.'

At quarter to four the telegrams of mobilization were handed in at the Central Telegraph Office in Paris.

Edward Spears, a young British cavalry officer, found the Boulevard Saint-Germain astonishingly quiet that afternoon: few passers-by and no cabs. What on earth was going on? That was the second woman he had met hurrying past apparently in tears. 'Traffic in Paris has never been slow, but now the motors fairly whizzed past driven by men with strained, set faces.' He turned back. And there, on the walls of the Palais Bourbon, still damp from the billposter's brush and shining under the sun, was the order for general mobilization:

Armée de Terre et Armée de Mer.
ORDRE DE MOBILISATION GÉNÉRALE

For a while, then, in the intense heat of that afternoon, the whole of Paris seemed to hold its breath. There were no taxis.

The Métro did not run. The buses were requisitioned to carry meat to the army.

To young officers, shy of unfamiliar accoutrements, the idea of walking through the streets in boots, sabre and uniform was disagreeable. One of them was lucky enough to find a fiacre. But hardly had he got in when a woman with two children, a great deal of luggage and a canary in a cage, begged him to give her a lift. It was impossible to refuse. After a bit the perspiring lieutenant caught sight of a taxi and rushed to stop it: 'State of siege!' he cried. 'I requisition you.' The taxi-driver submitted without a struggle.

In Paris, in Berlin, all over Europe, the young men went to join their regiments as gaily as if they were going to a picnic. There was shouting, laughter and, almost without stopping, the singing of national songs. In the barracks in Paris there was so much din that nobody heard the tocsin which, at four o'clock exactly, called the nation to arms in response to the 'white telegram' from the Ministry of War. At four o'clock in St. Malo, 'a fine misty day in a seaside summer', the novelist Colette heard it: 'There was a crowd round the beadle with the drum who was reading; nobody listened to what he said because we knew what it was.'

The response to the call to arms was for the most part gratifying in every country. Paléologue was told by a spy that amid the patriotic enthusiasm in St. Petersburg no further strikes were likely. The French General Staff had expected that thirteen reservists out of every hundred would fail to turn up. They were delighted to find that less than 1·5 per cent were missing. Mobilization had come like a holiday, on a day of holiday weather.

In the Soho restaurants in London, French, German and Austrian waiters who had been working amicably side by side abandoned their customers, rolled up their aprons, put on their hats and departed, exchanging black looks.

Mr. C. M. Houghton travelled from Yorkshire to Paris that day. He was a young Esperantist on his way to an International

Esperanto Congress due to meet in the Palais Gaumont Cinema next day. More than 3700 Esperantists were expected to turn up for it. On the quayside at Dieppe the British party saw the mobilization notices and realized that something was afoot. At the Gare St. Lazare they were confronted by a large notice in their favourite language: The International Esperanto Congress would not take place.

Mr. Houghton took the next boat back to England. Dr. Zamenhof, author of the language, on his way to Paris from Russia, was turned back in Germany.[1]

Crowds in the Unter den Linden in Berlin. Speeches in front of Josty's Konditorei. War would be exhilarating, heroic and, of course, victorious. It would also be brief. This expectation had the authority of Moltke's entourage, who said that the war could not last longer than forty days. In the late evening, while it was still light, a procession in military formation marched to the Chancellor's palace where, under poor Bethmann's windows, they sang 'Heil Dir in Siegeskranz'. The time for sober diplomacy was over. The spirit of the mob, roused and released, had invaded the quiet rooms of the ministers, who began to look with impatience on the 'paper-work' which stood, a barrier more flimsy every hour, between the warrior and his mission.

The spirit of the mob shone exultantly in the eyes of a sombre, ungainly young Austrian who stood in the crowd on the Odeonsplatz in Munich. Later on, in the quiet of his room, Adolf Hitler threw himself on his knees and thanked God to be alive at such an hour.

. . . . . .

1. 'Individuals and conducted parties set out from all over the Continent full of hope, only to be met on the 1st of August by the ominous word Mobilization. Many of the travellers experienced considerable difficulties in reaching their homes; some were thrown into internment camps, others returned by long and devious routes. Dr. Zamenhof stopped at Cologne, and after hurrying to the Russian border found it closed. He then had to travel through Sweden and Finland, finally reaching Warsaw via St. Petersburg.'—E. D. Durrant, *The Language Problem.*

More anxious than Pourtalès, Paul Cambon haunted Sir Edward Grey's room in the Foreign Office. There he found little comfort. The Foreign Secretary told him that France must make up her mind for herself what she should do now that Germany had declared war on Russia. France was bound to Russia by her alliance; Britain had purposely kept clear of all alliances. She did not even know the terms of the Franco-Russian treaty. Cambon, who was under frightful strain, who knew of the discussions in the Cabinet and knew where Grey's personal feelings lay, broke out emotionally: 'I refuse to transmit this message to Paris. It would fill France with indignation.' What if the German fleet were to steam into the Channel and attack France's defenceless coasts? Coasts, he might have added, which were defenceless because of a naval agreement with Britain.

'That would change public opinion in Britain,' Grey admitted. Was he giving a promise, or was it less than that?

The Frenchman desperately wanted something more precise. But Grey had gone as far as he could, and further than he should. He pointed out that, so long as he did not give Germany a guarantee of British neutrality, the German fleet would not risk entering the Channel and thus laying itself open to annihilation.

Grey's position was one of extreme delicacy. By failing to keep his colleagues steadily in touch with the development of foreign policy he had won freedom of manœuvre for himself. But it was a freedom exercised in semi-darkness and open to challenge. At some stage he had, half consciously, surrendered to the ruling faction in the Foreign Office which saw Germany as Britain's sole enemy. But this opinion was not shared by half of Grey's colleagues in the Liberal Cabinet and half of the Liberal party. Grey was conducting what would later be called a bi-partisan policy, for it found a completer acceptance among the Conservative opposition than on the government benches.

Moreover, almost the whole influence and moral weight of the Liberal press was eloquently against him: C. P. Scott and C. E. Montague in the *Manchester Guardian*, H. W. Massingham and H. N. Brailsford in the *Nation*, A. G. Gardiner in the *Daily News* and F. H. Hirst in the *Economist*. All of these powerful voices were raised against intervention. Only in the *Westminster Gazette* could Grey count on steady support, from J. A. Spender.

Day after day the *Manchester Guardian* pounded the government's policy, known, guessed or suspected, in nervous prose sharpened with a Liberal philosophy of unimpeachable orthodoxy. A few hours before Grey's emotional encounter with Cambon the *Daily News* had hinted ominously that 'pressure on the government from those obscure forces that make for war is heavy and growing heavier'.

The *Nation*, an intellectual weekly with some influence, found it 'safe to say that there has been no crisis in which the political opinion of the English people has been so definitely opposed to war as it is at the moment. A minister who led this country into war would cease to lead the Liberal party.' It called on the committee of the National Liberal Federation to meet at once; it spoke severely of Churchill's 'needless, dangerous and ill-advised naval precautions'.

And on that same morning *The Times*, which the *Manchester Guardian* denounced as a betrayer of Britain, printed, with what reluctance can only be surmised, a closely reasoned letter from Norman Angell. He was the author of *The Great Illusion*, a famous polemic against the unprofitable nature of war in the modern age. What Angell said would command a wide audience. And what he said on that cool Saturday in August was plain enough:

> The object and effect of our entering this war would be to ensure the victory of Russia and her Slavonic allies. Will a dominant Slavonic federation of, say, 200,000,000 autocratically governed people with a very rudimentary civilization but heavily equipped for military aggression be a less dangerous factor in Europe than a dominant Germany of 65,000,000? . . . The last war we fought on the Continent was for the purpose of preventing the growth of Russia. We are now asked to fight for the purpose of promoting it.

The tone was moderate; the appeal was to reason and to self-interest. Thousands must have read and recognized the cogency of the argument. Yet they would read with a sense of futility.

In *The Times* office Lord Northcliffe called a conference of his editors. The government, he told them, was going to rat. What should they do? 'Go bald-headed against it,' said Wickham Steed. Marlowe, editor of the *Daily Mail*, thought the country would never forgive a direct attack on the government at such a moment.

The German Consul-General in London, von Ranke, announced in *The Times* that the Kiel Canal, reopened only a few weeks earlier after a deepening operation which had cost £11,000,000, was closed to merchant shipping. Not far above this advertisement were two others, one seeking 'Companion gun in excellent mixed shoot in Essex'; the other less explicit: 'Pauline. Alas, it cannot be, but I will dash into the great venture with all that pride and spirit an ancient race has given me— A. L'A.'

The Board of Agriculture in London estimated that Britain had four months' supply of wheat. In a week the price of the grain had risen five shillings a sack. Newspapers spoke, with tolerance, of food-hoarding. The Bank Rate, which had doubled to 8 per cent the day before, now rose to 10.

Commissioned by *Comœdia* to write a series of descriptive articles, Guillaume Apollinaire spent the height of the season at Deauville, accompanied by his friend Rouveyre, the illustrator. The beach was charming; the crowd cosmopolitan; the women pretty. If only the political news, which, as they noticed, grew every day a shade more ominous, had not kept eating into the smooth and glistening surface of that Norman holiday!

One day the two young men became aware that faces had grown longer. The once-gay public had serious preoccupations. By perceptible degrees the crowd on the front was thinning.

While they sat in the Casino watching the tango, that tense and difficult dance imported from South America, news came which scattered the frivolous crowd. Mobilization.

Apollinaire and Rouveyre set off for Paris at daybreak, passing on the way countless racing cars making for Deauville where the annual automobile races were about to be held. At Lisieux they paused under a street-lamp to mend a puncture. The lamp went out. 'An omen of war?' asked Rouveyre.

When Apollinaire reached Montparnasse a procession of flushed patriots was marching up the Boulevard towards the Lion de Belfort. Montparnasse had been given a bad reputation by chauvinist writers as a haunt of cosmopolitans, anarchists, Cubists, in short of every element out of sympathy with the nation's bellicose mood. Outside the Rotonde, the mob roared, 'Shoot the traitors!' reflecting the mental confusion of the President of the Salon d'Automne who, on hearing that war had broken out, said, 'This will mean the end of Cubism.'

Apollinaire, half Russian, half Italian, wholly Parisian, described the journey in a poem:

> We arrived in Paris
> At the moment when the mobilization posters were going up
> And my comrade and I understood then
> That the little motor-car had brought us into a new
> Epoch
> And, though we were both grown up,
> We had just been born . . .

George Braque was mobilized (later on he was severely wounded). Marinetti, the apostle of Futurism, was arrested in Italy for publicly tearing up seven Austrian flags.

In Cetinje, the village capital of Montenegro, parliament declared its support for Serbia. When King Nicholas begged them to show some common sense the members retired to the cafés, grumbling. 'God is my witness,' Nicholas declared to an Austrian diplomat, 'I never willed this war.'

That evening, while Winston Churchill was playing a rubber of bridge at Admiralty House, a red Foreign Office box arrived. He opened it. Germany had declared war on Russia. Churchill asked Sir Max Aitken to take over his hand.[1] He changed his dress-coat and went out. Crossing the Horse Guards Parade, he entered 10 Downing Street by the garden gate. The Prime Minister was in the drawing-room with Grey, Haldane, Lord Crewe and other ministers. Churchill told them that he meant to mobilize the fleet at once in spite of the Cabinet's decision that there was no need to do so: 'I would take full personal responsibility to the Cabinet the next morning.' Although the Prime Minister said nothing, the First Lord read approval in his face. Churchill left the house with Grey, who said: 'You should know I have just done a very important thing. I have told Cambon that we shall not allow the German fleet to come into the Channel.' Grey had not gone as far as that, although he may have thought he had done so.

Churchill walked back to the Admiralty and issued the orders which mobilized the British fleet.

In the early hours of the morning the Kaiser was awakened by his valet Schulz with the news that his aide-de-camp, Colonel von Mutius, sought an audience. Wearing a military greatcoat over his underclothes, the Kaiser read the telegram which Mutius brought. Georgie in London explained that Lichnowsky had got things wrong. Britain would guarantee the French neutrality only if Germany were neutral towards Russia as well as France.

The Kaiser called his Chief of the General Staff to the palace: 'Now you can do as you wish. March into Luxembourg.'

Moltke's agony was over.

But it seems that he never quite recovered from the crisis of that day. Perhaps it was too much, on top of a double Carlsbad cure. At any rate, in ten days' time the head of the Kaiser's military cabinet, General von Lyncker, asked Falkenhayn if he would be willing to take over Moltke's duties in case of a break-down: 'Of course, I cannot say otherwise than Yes.'[2]

1. It was a bad hand.
2. He did so a month later.

*Nous autres civilizations, nous savons
maintenant que nous sommes mortelles.'*
PAUL VALÉRY

14

Luncheon was Late at
Number Ten

Sunday, 2 August

THE centre of the European crisis, moving westwards, came
to rest over London. In travelling it had subtly changed its
nature, adapting itself to the environment of the people it had
come to visit.

In London the situation was more complex and undependable
than on the Continent. There was public opinion, raising itself
obstinately against the assumption that Britain was obliged to be
swept along on any continental flood. There were newspapers
powerfully declaiming on issues of principle—Principle! There
was Parliament, which had listened but had not spoken yet. And
there was the Cabinet, which had still, if it could, to make up its
collective mind and deliver its collective judgement to the people.

In crossing the English Channel the crisis had acquired
confusing and troublesome moral attributes.

Two hours before Herbert Asquith greeted his ministers in the Cabinet room of 10 Downing Street, the first blood had been shed in Europe.

Soon after nine on that Sunday morning came the first clash of French and German troops. What exactly happened depends upon which of two conflicting narratives is to be trusted. The German account has a proper note of *furor Teutonicus*.

Lieutenant Meyer of the Uhlans, on reconnaissance, saw two sentries on the road near Dille. 'Swift as lightning, and with the first stroke of his sabre, he despatched a French infantryman while Soldier-first-class Heitze thrust his lance into the chest of the other.'

The French have a different recollection of the encounter: A post of the 44th French Infantry Regiment was quietly taking its soup in a farm kitchen when the daughter of the house, who had gone out to fetch water from a well, returned, crying: 'Help! The Prussians are here!' The German lieutenant opened fire on the French and hit Corporal Peugeot, who, before falling dead, was able to bring the lieutenant down with a bullet. Only one of the eight Germans in the patrol regained Mulhouse. . . .

In a morning of brilliant sunshine all the young men in Berlin suddenly appeared in field grey. In the Prussian War Ministry, General Falkenhayn, wearing a close-fitting tunic of white drill, was relaxed and confident. Military maps were spread on the table before him. 'I have finished my job,' he said, with a shrug of his broad shoulders. And indeed there was an impression in Berlin that morning of some machine very powerful and very smooth-running, which had started moving, which would gain momentum almost effortlessly and which could not be stopped by any power on earth save the command of the All-Highest himself.

A regiment of Uhlans rode across the Potzdammer Platz singing 'In der Heimat'. One or two women in the watching crowd seemed inclined to be tearful. 'There is no harm at all,' said one elderly diplomat who noticed this, 'in the people having their little share of trouble.' The ordeals of the diplomats were, for the moment, almost at an end. And this was what the diplomats had created by their travail—this grim yet thrilling cavalcade of strong young men with lances riding on gleaming horses towards distant battlefields as yet unnamed.

In another city a similar spectacle of riders and fine horses was viewed from a different angle. On the platform of the Eiffel Tower soldiers kept a look-out for the approach of German aircraft.

Below, in its vast amphitheatre, the city glistened in the sunshine. Its streets were quieter than usual. One did not need to be very imaginative to feel that a hush had fallen and that the proudest capital in Europe was waiting for the onset of some danger, some crisis, some decision which would change the fate of the world. Paris looked what it was, the appropriate theatre of a tremendous drama.

Immediately below, 985 feet down through the lucid air, a regiment of cuirassiers left the École Militaire. Tiny figures in dark blue and scarlet on elegant horses, the sunlight stroked their swords and lit tiny sparks of silver and gold on helmets and breastplates. As they passed, two by two, with the tricolour at their head, the small heads of pedestrians uncovered. They rode slowly towards the Pont de l'Alma and, gaining the distant bank of the river, were lost to view.

It was the beginning of a march which would take those cavalrymen to the neighbourhood of Namur and then, retreating southwards before a grey tide of invasion, fringed by Uhlans like those crossing the Potzdammer Platz, back to the river which they had just crossed. By that time the horses would have lost their brilliant sheen and many of them would have lost their armoured and helmeted riders. In that distant, unimaginable extremity, the cuirassiers would be called upon to make a supreme effort.

The toy soldiers of the École Militaire, those bright and touching miniatures moving over the nursery floor of Paris, were, though they did not know it, riding to the Battle of the Marne.

A crowd of some thousands, gathered at the Bismarck monument in Konigs Platz, heard one of the Kaiser's court preachers pray for victory. They sang devoutly some sturdy Lutheran hymns. The Crown Prince, Kaiser Wilhelm's eldest son, drove several times to the offices of the General Staff. Each time, it was noticed, His Imperial Highness was wearing a different uniform.

In Dresden General von Hausen, who had just been called on to assume command of the Third Army, received communion with his wife from Court Preacher Dr. Friederich.

After taking communion at St. Paul's Mrs. Asquith dropped her daughter Elizabeth in Downing Street and walked across the Horse Guards Parade to the German Embassy. She found her friend Princess Lichnowsky lying on her green sofa. The Princess's eyes were red with weeping. The Prince walked up and down the room, wringing his hands. 'Oh! say there is surely not going to be war!' (Even in the stress of that moment Mrs. Asquith noticed that he pronounced the word to rhyme with 'far'.) 'Dear Mrs. Asquith, can *nothing* be done to prevent it?' The Prime Minister's wife put her arms round the Princess. Both ladies burst into tears.

'Have I not always loathed the Kaiser and his brutes of friends,' cried Mechtilde Lichnowsky, waving distractedly to the sky over St. James's Park visible through the window. 'One thousand times I have said the same. I will never cross his threshold again.'

'He is ill-informed—impulsive and must be *mad*,' said the Prince apologetically. 'He answers none of my telegrams!' His wife added bitterly, 'Ah, that brutal hard war-party of ours makes men fiends.'

The Prince wept. Mrs. Asquith left. Lunch was late at No. 10.

The Cabinet, which had met at eleven, was still sitting at a quarter to two.

From his chair in the middle of the long table with its covering of green baize, the Prime Minister glanced this way and that at his colleagues. Before him was the garden, behind him the white marble mantelpiece, the clock, the portrait of Sir Robert Walpole by Van Loo. Asquith knew that only half of his ministers were of the opinion that Britain should go to war if France were attacked. Prominent among the war party was Winston Churchill, 'in tearing spirits' at the prospect of battle. The Prime Minister thought that this showed a certain lack of imagination in the young First Lord of the Admiralty. Lord Crewe was wise and equable. With Sir Edward Grey, Asquith was in agreement over the whole range of the problem. The Prime Minister could count on the loyalty of Haldane, Herbert Samuel and Reginald McKenna. At the opposite pole, Lord Morley and John Burns were steadfastly and, in all likelihood, immovably against war. Between were the doubters, by far the most important of these the Radical Chancellor of the Exchequer, David Lloyd George. Asquith observed him closely. 'Lloyd George is nervous,' he decided. It was, as the Prime Minister knew very well, the nervousness of a man who thought with his ears as well as his brain, who listened to the murmur of the crowds as well as to the impulses of conscience and the calculations of policy.

To this divided group of Liberal statesmen, which included imperialists, near-pacifists and pro-Germans, was put the question: What answer should Sir Edward Grey give to the French ambassador, Paul Cambon, who had inquired what Britain would do if the German fleet attacked French ships or ports in the Channel? Grey wished to say that the British navy would open fire.

Lord Morley led the opposition to Grey. He was seventy-five, frail and very distinguished; disagreeable and self-righteous. Lord Rosebery had called him 'a petulant spinster'. He might have been Foreign Secretary at one time, but he had a wife who had lived under his roof before marriage and thus was debarred from receiving the wives of ambassadors.

Was Germany really the 'great aggressor', as Grey alleged? Lord Morley took leave to doubt it. What about Russia? What if Russia were to be the ultimate victor? 'Have you ever thought?' he asked the ministers earnestly. 'If Germany is beaten and Austria is beaten it is not England and France that will emerge pre-eminent in Europe. It will be Russia. Will that be good for Western civilization?'

Lord Morley's voice was light and precise. But tremendous realities hung in the balance that day. The most momentous decision ever taken in that room must soon be made. The old man's querulous voice was weighted with the moral passion of generations of Liberals. The Liberals who had detested the Boer War (like Lloyd George), who had responded to Gladstone's fervour against oppression and imperialism, and who had as one of the favourite targets for their disapproval the Russia of Tsar, Cossack, knout and Siberia. Compared with that tyranny, even bombastic, restless and dangerous Germany seemed a less dismal power. Morley knew that he was calling to ancient and deep-seated prejudices in his hearers. But on how many men round the table could he really count? How many of them had the steadfastness of mind and the fire of conviction to see the business through to a break, and beyond?

A night or two earlier, in Lulu Harcourt's room at the House, he had met Earl Beauchamp and some other ministers, all of whom were roused against any attempt to stiffen the Entente with France and Russia into an alliance. The partisans of neutrality were confident that they could count on eight or nine votes in the Cabinet, half its members, enough to destroy Asquith's government.

Arriving at No. 10, Morley had run into the 'splendid condottiere at the Admiralty', Churchill, whom he loved dearly. 'Winston,' he said, 'we've beaten you after all.' Churchill grinned cheerfully and said nothing. And Morley had no sure faith in the staunchness of the peace party. He knew how powerful were the temptations of place and popularity. He looked with a placidly sceptical eye on his friends in the neutralist group. In his own opposition to Grey's policy there was something mild as well as something implacable; a tincture of resignation in his rejection. Lord Morley's was the opposition of an old man.

He argued that the Cabinet had known nothing of the extent of the military conversations with the French. Even Grey had kept himself ostentatiously ignorant of them. How then could it be said that Britain was committed in honour or law?

He might have brought back to the memory of the others the circumstances in which the talks had begun, and recalled how Asquith had told Grey in 1911 that these conversations were 'rather dangerous' since the French might be encouraged to make plans on the assumption of British collaboration. Grey, at that time, had answered soothingly: There would be consternation in Paris if the talks were not continued. No doubt an expectation of British support had been raised, but 'I do not see how that can be helped'.

A year afterwards, when the news was broken to the Cabinet that the talks had been going on, ministers had suspected that there was something to conceal. And Grey had written a letter to Cambon renewing his claim—in which he must have believed—that Britain's hands remained free. There was no engagement to co-operate in war. In a crisis, both sides, France and Britain, would take into consideration the plans which the soldiers had concerted and would decide 'what effect should be given them'. In 1912 that formula had seemed satisfactory. On that Sunday morning in 1914 it wore a less substantial air. The longer Morley looked at it, the flimsier seemed the safeguard it offered to the Cabinet's power to determine Britain's policy in freedom.

Some ministers, Lloyd George among them, felt the resentment of men who had allowed themselves, through stupidity, lazy-mindedness or excess of trust, to be cheated out of their full liberty of decision. They claimed that a web of obligations, which they had been assured were *not* obligations, had been spun round them while they slept. But they knew they had not slept all the time. Like Grey, who had deliberately stayed 'ignorant' of the outcome of the military talks with France, they had deliberately shut their eyes. But not all of them, and not all the time.

Morley might insist on his innocence, but Lord Haldane could produce from a red box of Committee of Imperial Defence papers a memorandum of General Ewart's of 1910 discussing a proposed concentration of the British expeditionary force at Maubeuge. And at the foot of the paper was the minute: 'Doubtful if I ought to approve of this. But I suppose it's in the interests of European peace.' It was in Morley's handwriting.

There was another occasion, too, when Britain had allowed assurances to be given to the French. One day in November 1911 Cambon had sent a message to his Prime Minister in Paris, 'In the event of Germany attacking France or wilfully breaking off the negotiations, British public opinion would side with France and would enable the British government to support France.' Grey had read this message to a Cabinet at which Harcourt and Morley were present. And none of the ministers had repudiated it. Could it be argued that the formula referred only to the temporary diplomatic crisis of 1911?

The incident was apparently forgotten by the ministers who brooded over the far graver crisis of 1914.

When at last the long Cabinet came to an end it appeared that Grey had carried the day. He was authorized to tell Cambon that if the German fleet came into the Channel to undertake hostile operations against France the British fleet would give France all the protection that it could.

The neutralists had suffered a severe tactical defeat, although the main issue was still undecided. Pressing forward to a war in Europe in which Britain would be ranged at France's side, Asquith, Grey, Haldane and Churchill might find themselves deserted by a great mass of Liberal M.P.s and dependent on Conservative votes in the House of Commons, as Grey was already dependent on Conservative support in the press. There could be no relish for a Liberal Prime Minister in going to war in such circumstances.

Before the Cabinet broke up, John Burns announced that he would resign. Asquith, playing desperately but suavely for time, for something to happen which he believed would happen, asked him to postpone his final decision until the Cabinet met again at half past six. Burns agreed.

Lloyd George and John Simon drove Morley to lunch at Beauchamp's house. All three were in favour of resignation. Lewis Harcourt, Pease and Samuel arrived soon afterwards. The general feeling among them was that Burns in resigning had chosen the right path.

Joseph A. Pease was a coal-owner from the North, fifty-four years of age; a Quaker of a family illustrious in the sect, yet one on whom its restrictions sat lightly enough for him to keep a pack of beagles. He was, however, President of the Peace Society.

Before arriving at Beauchamp's he had lunched with the Prime Minister who had, jokingly, begged him to keep the conspirators in Belgrave Square out of mischief.

Something in the tone of Pease's remarks that afternoon warned Morley that the President of the Peace Society would not be wholly averse to having a hand in Armageddon.

Lewis Harcourt, who did not object to the nickname of 'Lulu', was a rich, indulgent man of fifty-one with an American wife and strong aesthetic tastes. He was believed to have a strain of Plantagenet blood. He was charming, fastidious and not unduly burdened with principle. He lived well in his house in Berkeley Square, and even more agreeably in a country place near Oxford. A Liberal journalist had said of him: 'He loves the intricacies of the campaign more than the visionary gleam.' He had adored his father, Sir William Harcourt, whom once he had hoped to make Prime Minister, a dream which Morley had helped to shatter. Lulu despised Morley. Yet in policy Harcourt belonged, as Morley did and Lloyd George also, to the stream of Radical thought which had opposed the Boer War. Once he had described himself to a German ambassador as 'an extreme Germanophile', and it had only been half joking. In 1912 he had declared in public that he could conceive of no circumstances in which 'continental operations by our troops would not be a crime against the people of this country'. But, with his easy-going nature, Harcourt seemed scarcely the ideal leader of a last stand for extreme principle in an hour of intense emotional strain.

What of the key-figure in the schism which seemed to be tearing the government apart?

During that afternoon at Beauchamp's, Simon whispered excitedly to Morley, 'I think I've got Ll.G.' Morley was unconvinced. A man who thought he had 'got' the Chancellor of the Exchequer was sanguine indeed! Samuel, whose main concern was to keep the Liberal Government in being, shared Morley's scepticism. When he met Asquith later in the afternoon the question was put to him, 'What will Lloyd George do?' Samuel, who had heard the Chancellor of the Exchequer insist that he meant to resign, replied, 'I do not know.'

Since Asquith was resolute for the interventionist policy of which he, Grey and Haldane were the protagonists, he faced the prospect that war might have to be waged by a Coalition government drawing most of its strength from the Conservative opposition. He did not think well of coalitions, nor was he impressed by the quality of the opposition front bench. What Prime Minister ever is? But he knew that he could count on Conservative support for intervention. He had in his pocket a letter from the Conservative leader Bonar Law, who had written after consultation with his chief lieutenants, Lord Lansdowne and Austen Chamberlain. Bonar Law wrote to the Prime Minister: 'It would be fatal to the honour and security of the United Kingdom to hesitate in supporting France and Russia at the present juncture.'

A Coalition with the Conservatives? And Lloyd George, the dazzling, devious idol of the Radical masses, as leader of an opposition pledged to peace! The prospect was not an alluring one for a Liberal Prime Minister who knew that the split in his Cabinet reflected a deep division in Parliament.

Asquith was somewhat comforted by the news that the great demonstration against war being held at that moment in Trafalgar Square was not a success. Keir Hardie had spoken from the plinth of the Nelson Column. War, he had shouted, in his strong Scottish accent, would be the greatest calamity the world had ever seen.

But there had been as much enthusiasm and more singing from a patriotic counter-demonstration gathered round the statue of Charles I. This, by chance, was reinforced by a body of French reservists carrying tricolours and on their way to Victoria Station. A reporter from the *Manchester Guardian* noted with satisfaction that a sudden squall of rain brought the outburst of jingoism to a sudden and damp conclusion.

When the weather allowed, the approaches to Downing Street were thronged with the idle and the curious who greeted ministers with welcoming cheers. The London public, it seemed, was not wholly dedicated to the ideal of peace.

Lord Morley spent two hours in his club, a prey to deep and melancholy reflections on men and affairs. To hold a minority opinion was one thing, to resign from a Cabinet quite another. 'No fugitive Sabbath musing was it, either then or since, that filled my mind.'

When Grey had brought the Cabinet hard against the issue of peace and war, of neutrality and intervention, he had reinforced his own policy with the threat of resignation. Morley could do no less. He saw no sign of a leader for the peace party strong enough to stand against Asquith and Grey and the 'cohesion of office'. Lloyd George? His attitude was equivocal, the mainspring of his thought hidden from view. On the whole, Lord Morley was not inclined to search for the clues to Lloyd George's likely course on the higher levels of human impulse. The Chancellor's 'stock' was low. He might think that, as leader of a peace faction, he would find a way back to popular favour. On the other hand, the deliberate disruption of the Liberal party was a prospect to daunt the most excitable of Radical politicians.

By the time he made his way through the crowds in Whitehall to attend the resumed Cabinet at half past six, Lord Morley knew the path that he for one would follow.

·　　·　　·　　·　　·

Soon after Cabinet, Grey asked the French ambassador, Paul Cambon, to call at the Foreign Office. For Cambon it was a time of intense strain—'three days like three centuries'. He had seen Wickham Steed of *The Times* at midday and spoken bitterly to him. 'I do not know whether we shall have to strike the word honour out of the English vocabulary.' What would Sir Edward have to say after this long and trying Cabinet?

The Foreign Secretary told him of the Cabinet's decision to use the fleet to prevent the German navy from bombarding the French coast.

Cambon was careful to hide his satisfaction. But he had no doubt that an important obstacle had been passed, perhaps the decisive one. Later on, he said: 'The game was won. A great country does not make war by halves.' But Cambon could hardly feel this degree of certainty on that August afternoon. For what if the Kaiser's fleet left the French coast alone? What if the German army, in its invasion of France, carefully avoided Calais and Boulogne?

As the advance guard of General Tulff von Tscheepe's German army corps marched through the streets of Luxembourg, they were surprised to see an elderly man in the uniform of an officer of the Prussian Guard, standing to attention on the pavement. They would have been even more surprised had they known who he was. . . .

Eight years before, Germany had been swept by a gale of laughter over the exploit of a shoemaker and gaolbird named Wilhelm Voigt. He had bought the uniform of a Prussian officer in a second-hand clothes shop. Wearing this, he had assumed command of a passing detachment of soldiers and marched on the town hall of Koepenick. There he arrested the mayor and seized the money in the municipal cashbox.

For demonstrating in this unconventional way the prestige of the Prussian uniform, the 'Captain of Koepenick' was sentenced to a term of imprisonment—and released after a year. He made

173

some money by showing himself in the music halls, selling signed photographs, etc. One day he retired and bought a little house in Luxembourg. . . .

A hand rose smartly to the brim of a helmet as the German colours advanced into the streets of Luxembourg. The officer in command of the marching soldiers gave the order, 'Eyes—*right*!' Thus, on the eve of battle, the German army saluted its old tormentor, the 'Captain of Koepenick'.[1]

In the Treasury Basil Blackett struggled against the sinister desire of the joint-stock banks to suspend specie payments. He was profoundly dubious about the soundness on this issue of his chief, Mr. Lloyd George. Casting about for reinforcements, Blackett sent a cry for help to Cambridge, to his friend John Maynard Keynes. There was an economist one could count on to write a cogent and graceful minute!

When Keynes received the summons he was faced by a problem of transport. It was Sunday and trains were few and slow. He appealed to his brother-in-law, A. V. Hill, who had a motor bicycle and sidecar. In this the pair set off for London. As they neared Whitehall, both rider and passenger recoiled from the impropriety of arriving at the Treasury on Sunday afternoon mounted on such a vehicle.

Keynes finished the journey on foot.

In St. Petersburg, at three o'clock, an imposing ceremony took place in the Winter Palace.

The St. George's Hall, an immense room with pure white marble walls and columns richly embellished with gilded bronze, runs parallel to the Neva Quay. In it five or six thousand persons were assembled. The court was in gala costumes, the women

1. Wilhelm Voigt, died 4 January 1922; is buried in Luxembourg, where his grave is piously maintained. (*La Vie Quotidienne en Allemagne au temps de Guillaume II*. Pierre Bertaux. Hachette. 1962.)

wearing on their heads the crescent-shaped kakoshnik orna-
mented with jewels. The court Arabs, maintained since the time
of the Empress Elizabeth, wore white turbans, baggy trousers
and Turkish slippers. They were Christians brought from
Ethiopia as a demonstration of the universal claims of the Orthodox Church. The Gardes à Cheval and the Chevaliers Gardes,
who would normally have been resplendent figures in black
and scarlet with gleaming cuirasses and double-eagle helmets,
were, like the other soldiers, in drab-coloured service uniforms.

In the middle of the hall an altar had been erected and the
miraculous ikon of the Virgin of Kazan had been brought. Before
it, Prince Kutusov had prayed long and fervently when he was
about to take over command of the Russian army in 1812.

In a deathly silence the imperial procession entered the hall and
took up their places to the left of the altar. Paléologue, the only
foreigner present, was opposite the Tsar. During the mass, which
was long and beautifully sung, the Emperor prayed with ardour.
The Tsarina's face was rigid, her eyes glassy. The court chaplain
read the Tsar's message to his people, explaining why the war was
inescapable, appealing to the nation to put out all its energies.
Then the Tsar, going forward to the altar, took up the Gospel
in his right hand. Grave and composed, speaking slowly, he took
the same oath that Alexander I had taken in 1812: 'Officers of my
guard here present, I salute and bless in you all my army.
Solemnly I swear that I will not conclude peace as long as there is
one enemy on the soil of our country.' A wave of cheering, which
lasted for ten minutes, shook the hall.

It was not perhaps the moment to remember that there was no
early likelihood of either Germans or Austrians violating the
sacred soil of Russia. The expectation was of an entirely different
nature. Poincaré was only echoing the general confidence of the
Tsar's high command when he assured a French minister, 'The
Russians will be in Berlin by All Saints' Day.' But in the enthusiasm and fever of that afternoon in the white marble gallery by
the Neva men were uplifted by the stern sense of national danger,
the solemn call to sacrifice. The Grand Duke Nicholas crushed

M. Paléologue to his bosom. Cries of *'Vive la France'* broke out everywhere.

The Tsar, from the balcony of the palace, greeted a crowd assembled outside carrying banners, ikons and portraits of the Little Father. Immediately, thousands went down on their knees and sang the national anthem. Paléologue returned to his embassy, quite exhausted by these grandiose scenes.

In Biarritz, about the same time, Count Witte, former Prime Minister of Russia, prophesied that disaster would be the outcome of the war which he had steadfastly opposed.

When Asquith's Cabinet met again, Grey repeated to his colleagues what he had said to Cambon. Burns repeated his decision to resign. Asquith asked him to stay for a talk after the others had gone. As the ministers filed out, Morley told the Prime Minister he, too, must go. 'One favour, at any rate, I would ask you,' said Asquith. 'Sleep on it.' 'Of course I will,' Morley answered. He left the Prime Minister to grapple—vainly—with the soul and conscience of John Burns.

The Liberal Cabinet still tottered on the brink of disintegration.

The American ambassador, Walter Page, had taken a cottage at Oakham in Surrey, an hour out of London. Affected, like every man of intelligence and feeling, by the seismic wave that was passing through the world, he sought calm in the open air.

'The stars are bright, the night is silent, the country quiet—as quiet as peace itself.' Page returned to the house and wrote: 'The Grand Smash is come. Last night the German ambassador at St. Petersburg handed the Russian Government a declaration of war. . . . Troops were marching through London at one o'clock this morning.'

Grey was dining with Haldane at Queen Anne's Gate when a red despatch box came in from the Foreign Office. It contained a message which they had been expecting.

Earlier that day the Belgian vice-consul at Cologne had arrived in a state of some excitement at the Foreign Ministry in

Brussels. He reported that since six o'clock in the morning troop trains had been leaving Cologne Station every three or four minutes. They were going, not south-west towards France, but towards Aix-la-Chapelle, in the direction of Belgium. Herr von Below, the German minister in Brussels, had, however, given positive assurances of the friendly attitude of Germany towards the Belgians in an interview to *Le Soir*. Captain Brinkmann, the German military attaché, asked another Brussels newspaper to deny categorically that Germany had declared war on France or even on Russia. Nor was it true that German troops had occupied the Grand Duchy of Luxembourg.

However, at seven in the evening Below called upon M. Davignon, the Foreign Minister. The interview lasted fifteen minutes; Below presented an ultimatum which Moltke himself had drafted a week before and which Jagow, Bethmann and other hands had amended.[1] The document had been in Brussels for five days in a sealed envelope. It invited Belgium to adopt a 'benevolent neutrality' to the German troops who would enter the country to meet the threat of a French invasion. Twelve hours were given for a reply.

The Belgian ministers decided to reject this dishonourable proposal. When the Council of State met at nine o'clock in the Royal Palace King Albert said, 'Our answer must be No.' The Council sat until four o'clock in the morning. The German ultimatum was rejected unanimously.

These events still hung in the balance when Grey and Haldane walked over to Downing Street with the news of the German ultimatum. Asquith agreed that mobilization of the army should be ordered. The next meeting of the British Cabinet would take place in a very different atmosphere from the last.

---

1. The ultimatum can hardly have come as a surprise to the well informed in any European capital. As far back as 1911, de-training platforms at Metz had been trebled in length; between Monshau and St. Vith, on the Belgian-German frontier, de-training space for 120,000 men had been provided. Tiny stations had platforms half a mile long. All this plainly suggested a German move into Belgium. E. D. Morel, '*Truth and the War*'.

> '*The cause is lack of capacity and not a deep and nefarious plan. Unfortunately, the effect remains the same.*'
>
> HEINRICH VON SYBELL, 1795

15

Sombre March of an Argument

Monday, 3 August

T HERE was warmth, with occasional bursts of sunshine, in London. The girls came out in their bright summer frocks. If they wore their hair down, tied in a big bow at the nape of the neck, they were called 'flappers' ('*backfisch*' in German). The young men, their companions, wore straw hats of one shape or another. The more elegant of them had well-pressed trousers displaying gaily coloured socks. They affected a drooping carriage and an air of boredom. These, known as the 'nuts', were celebrated in a song heard every night at the Palace Theatre in a revue, *The Passing Show*. It was sung by a popular performer of the time, Basil Hallam; its chorus began:

> 'I'm Gilbert the Filbert, the Nut with a K,
> The pride of Piccadilly, the blasé roué'

The song was still being sung on the London stage when many of the pride of Piccadilly already lay dead.

Ministers, gathering in Downing Street for the morning Cabinet, were startled and, in some cases, delighted by the boisterous greetings of the Bank Holiday crowds. In their grey top-hats and light frock-coats, the statesmen eyed one another appraisingly, wondering how many firm resolutions had survived the grave events of the night, the arguments of colleagues, the solicitings of ambition.

Half an hour before the meeting Lord Morley told Lloyd George, 'I'm going.' The Welshman gave him a glance that was part survey and part avowal. 'Don't be in a hurry,' he said. Morley decided that the Chancellor of the Exchequer had talked that morning, as he usually did, to the First Lord of the Admiralty, Churchill, and had drunk at that well of martial enthusiasm.

This was not, as it happened, the only influence at work on Lloyd George that morning. He had also received a minatory telegram from the oracle in Manchester. It said: 'Intense exasperation among leading Liberals here at prospect of government embarking on a war. No man who is responsible can lead us again. Scott.'

At that moment how difficult it was for a politician to sort out the just claims of duty, ambition and conscience!

While Lloyd George and Morley were having their brief exchange, Asquith was seeing the Conservative leaders in Commons and Lords, Andrew Bonar Law and Lord Lansdowne. They found the Prime Minister very tired, as well he might be, and waiting for definite news of the German invasion of Belgium, which he knew to be imminent. Until then he would play for time and keep his Cabinet together if he could.

As they filed into the Cabinet room at eleven o'clock, Lloyd George murmured in Morley's ear: 'I stay. It's Belgium.' Morley raised his fine eyebrows, without surprise. 'I go,' he said. Lloyd George protested: 'But that will put those of us who don't go in a hole!' Morley replied, 'German bullying of Belgium does not alter my aversion to the French entente policy.'

'It has changed Runciman's line and my own,' said Lloyd George.[1]

Two names fewer on the list of non-interventionists. A few hours earlier they had numbered ten or eleven, on the somewhat emotional reckoning of Harcourt.

John Simon had told the Prime Minister he would resign. It was a decision, and could not be changed. But since then Simon had breakfasted alone with Grey. Later on, in describing their conversation, he said that Grey's 'firmness of judgement, combined with his distress, were a great help to me. . . .' About others, yesterday strong in the non-interventionist faith, a strange silence reigned.

Asquith opened the Cabinet quietly and with some severity in his voice. 'I have this morning the resignation of four members of the Cabinet in my hands. Burns . . .' Then, with a glance at Morley, 'the one who is the greatest source of the moral authority of the government. . . . Simon and Lord Beauchamp. Many others, perhaps a majority of those present here, share their views.' What, then, should he do? Go to the King? Offer his resignation so that a new Prime Minister could be appointed? He allowed their minds to dwell on that before giving his opinion that the Conservatives did not have the men capable of meeting the crisis. A coalition? But coalitions have hardly ever turned out well.

In the silence that followed this dexterous performance eyes fell on Morley who was sitting next to Asquith. Morley asked what he could expect if he stayed on? Only everlasting wrangles with Winston (on whom the old man smiled benevolently). No. He would stand by his letter of resignation. And so, as it turned out, would Simon, who spoke briefly, with tears. Beauchamp too

1. In fact, Lloyd George's attitude to the war was equivocal for some time. In the days of August, he handled in the House of Commons the financial measures which war made necessary. But it was not until 19 September—six weeks after the outbreak of war—speaking in the Queen's Hall, in London, that he emerged as a zealot for the struggle and potentially a future war Prime Minister.

would stand firm. The Cabinet broke up. Those who were staying were in low spirits, those who meant to go experienced a lightening of the heart. So at least Morley and Beauchamp assured each other when they went to luncheon together at Beauchamp's house. The two ex-ministers gossiped amiably about who would succeed them. 'Who will take your office?' asked Beauchamp. 'Well,' said Morley with a smile, 'looking round the House of Lords I can see nobody but yourself, who held the office before me.' 'But how,' Beauchamp protested, 'could I take your place, sharing the opinion for which you have left it?'

How indeed! But of that particular question the last had not yet been spoken.

Morley went to his club for a while and then to the House of Lords. On the way there his eyes fell on the *Evening Standard* bill, 'On the brink of catastrophe'.

The Prime Minister drove to the House, loudly cheered by dense patriotic throngs which, as the afternoon advanced, filled Whitehall from Trafalgar Square to the Houses of Parliament. Everywhere little Union Jacks fluttered. Street vendors of the flags were doing a roaring trade.

Busy as he was, the Prime Minister had found time to send a message which caught Lord Kitchener on board the cross-Channel steamer at Dover, on the first leg of his journey back to Egypt. The Field Marshal was recalled to London on urgent business of state.

The House of Commons, as it stood in 1914, was an unimpressive debating chamber. It was more than a little cramped. The style of architecture was indifferent. All this could hardly be denied by anyone who surveyed it in a spirit of cool appraisal. Yet, it had magic, derived from what source who can say. It could become the worthy, majestic, inevitable setting of high occasions of public drama. For one of these—one of the most moving of all perhaps—the House was making ready in the early afternoon. When the Speaker's chaplain, in black silk and scarlet bands, sought to leave after saying prayers, he had some difficulty in fighting his way through the crowd. Chairs had been brought in for members, something that had not happened since Gladstone introduced his Home Rule·Bill.

Politically, the House was composed of equal numbers of Liberals and Conservatives, 272 of each. Asquith's majority depended upon forty-two Labour votes. There were also eighty-four Irish Nationalists who could, for the most part, be counted on to vote with the government.

Some time after half past three Sir Edward Grey, wearing a light grey summer suit, rose from the front bench. Since the speech was the climax of his career, since it was an occasion of sombre emotion; a triumph of intricate exposition and—by general consent—a turning-point in the history of Western Europe, careful scrutiny must be given to the matter as well as the manner of the address. It was not a simple declaration, for Sir Edward's task that afternoon was not a straightforward one. But it was made easier by the manifest gravity and nearness of the national danger. Faced by the dénouement, men were not disposed to question the steps by which it had been reached. And, even if they had been, there was no time to do so.

The Foreign Secretary's face was pale, his manner, as usual, cold. Yet his argument did not lack a degree of subtlety which an astuter orator might have envied, and overplayed.

He opened with an acknowledgement that British policy had failed: the peace of Europe could not be saved. There had not been enough time; there had been a disposition in some quarters to force the pace too rapidly. But the House was free to decide what Britain's attitude should be. It would do so untrammelled by secret engagement or obligation of honour. Until the day before, the government had given no promise to France of anything but diplomatic support.

He went on to explain how, in the year 1906, he had fallen in with a French argument. The argument was that should Britain ever decide that military support for France was justified then the decision would have little practical value if there were no previous military and naval conversations to give it substance. In other words, joint planning was needed if there was to be—even in hypothesis—joint action. So conversations had taken place, subject always to an understanding that neither government was committed to action, although each was obliged to consult the other should a threat to the general peace seem likely.

The silence in the chamber was complete, the tension acute when the Foreign Secretary read out the text of his letter to Cambon of November 1912. Parliament was learning for the first time of this crucial, if ambiguous, document. On that Bank Holiday afternoon in 1914 there was no time any longer to weigh its moral implications. In fact, the importance of the letter was not as great as it had been; the dubious safeguards of its phrases had only slight relevance in the grim political and moral crisis which now hung over Europe.

Grey pointed to one practical consequence of the talks with the French: their fleet was confined to the Mediterranean.

France, however, was in a different position from Britain; she had a treaty of alliance with Russia and, therefore, an obligation of honour. He did not even know the terms of the treaty, which in any case did not involve Britain.

Sir Edward's mood now changed from the cool historical to the direct emotional. He invited each member to look into his own heart and his own feelings and construe the extent of the obligation to France:

'I speak my personal view. The French fleet is now in the Mediterranean. The northern coasts of France are absolutely undefended. We could not stand aside with our arms folded if a foreign fleet battered and bombarded these undefended coasts. France is entitled to know and to know at once whether in the event of German attack on her coasts she could depend on British support. So I gave the pledge to M. Cambon yesterday afternoon. . . .'

Sir Edward added that the Germans had promised that their warships would not attack the French northern coast if Britain stayed neutral. But this 'was far too narrow an engagement for us'.

At this moment the more alert members of the House of Commons might have pricked up their ears. The Foreign Secretary's argument had been that Britain must defend the north coast of France because it had been denuded of defences, in agreement with Britain. Now Germany was promising not to attack that coast, yet Britain still would not promise to stay neutral. What then was the point of the appeal to the hearts and feelings of each? What was the relevance of the remark that 'we could not stand aside with our arms folded if a foreign fleet battered and bombarded these undefended coasts'? The most formidable mind among those alongside Grey on the government front bench noted, 'The sombre march of his argument carried this weighty admission forward in its stride.' In fact, the sombre march of Sir Edward's argument had already traversed several deep bogs and dense thickets of dialectic.

Starting from the proposition that the House was completely free in honour to decide its course, he had modulated suavely into the acknowledgement that this freedom had come to an end on the previous afternoon when he had given M. Cambon his pledge of naval support in the Channel which could only be repudiated by destroying the government. His listeners might have wondered why Sir Edward could not have waited a few hours longer and consulted them first. But no one spoke. And no one showed signs of restlessness when the Foreign Secretary sought to impose on the House his own notion of how a man of heart and feeling would respond to the battering and bombardment of the French coast. If anyone in Sir Edward's crowded audience resented this moral blackmail, he remained silent, cowed perhaps by the noble presence of the orator and his manifest sincerity.

Through the Entente, which had in some mysterious way assumed the force of a military obligation, Britain was tied to France, who, in turn, was tied by treaty to Russia. Over the interpretation of that treaty Britain had no influence; she did not even know its terms. The Foreign Secretary appeared actually to make a virtue of this admission. Yet inquiry would have revealed that the French government under Poincaré's influence had stretched to the limit its commitment to Russia; and that, through Paléologue's agency or blundering, it had failed to hold the Tsar back from the fatal decision to mobilize.

Dazed by the suddenness of their transition from the comfortable mists of delusion into a stark daylight in which war and power were dominant and the Entente was exposed as a one-sided alliance, Sir Edward's hearers were in no mood to analyse his argument. If its sombre march was, in fact, a stumbling and erratic progress, nobody seems to have noticed. The truth was that already, while Grey spoke, his apologia had lost some of its appositeness.

Every man in the House of Commons knew that Belgium had been handed an ultimatum by Germany, and that this transformed the moral and political situation. Belgium was small and undeniably pacific. She was ill-defended. In 1909, when the British public were indignant over Belgium's annexation of the Congo, the Belgians had feared a British invasion. In their alarm they had decided to strengthen the defences of Antwerp against attack from the sea. Eight big guns were ordered from Krupps. They were paid for, but, strangely enough, never delivered. Belgium's neutrality was an indispensable stone in the fabric of European order, a premise on which the security systems of France, Germany and Britain were built.

After Grey's skilful presentation of his French policy he passed on to Belgium. Here there was no need for a special effort of advocacy. Interest, conscience and heart in his audience were in one harmonious surge. The neutralists knew that, with this issue raised, their cause was lost. The white flags were falling. Defending his position to the last, C. E. Montague, who wrote the leading article in the *Manchester Guardian*, had attempted to apologize for Germany: 'Nor shall we apply a harsh judgement to what a man or nation does for life's sake.' Germany, threatened in the east by the Russian hordes, was entitled to defend herself in the west by any means available. Even on the government's back benches, listening in glowering silence to the Foreign Secretary, few men were willing to imitate the tolerance of the *Manchester*

Guardian. But Ramsay MacDonald, leader of the Labour group, was obstinate: 'We will offer him [Grey] ourselves if the country is in danger. But he has not persuaded me that it is.'

At twenty-five minutes to five the sitting was suspended. The House would meet again at seven, to hear more exact and—who could doubt it—graver tidings.

Wherever he went in the House of Lords Lord Morley heard of the tremendous impression Grey's speech had made. Helped, it may be, by the electricity in the air, the Foreign Secretary had scored a historic triumph of oratory.

The crowds in Whitehall were so dense by this time that extra police were called out to make way for the car that took the Prime Minister and his wife back to No. 10. Lloyd George noticed how 'warlike' the public was. It made an impression on him which he never forgot.

Sir Ernest Shackleton, an Antarctic explorer, lay off Margate in the ship *Endurance*. He was on his way to the South Pole. Going ashore, he read in the newspapers that Britain was about to mobilize. He telegraphed to the Admiralty at once, placing the resources of his expedition at the service of the country. But the First Lord declined the offer in one characteristic word: 'Proceed'.

Adolf Hitler, from his lodgings in Munich, sent an urgent and impassioned plea to King Ludwig of Bavaria begging to be allowed to enlist in a Bavarian regiment. If this appeal were granted (as it graciously was in due course) the wild-eyed exile from Vienna would be able to serve in the glorious German army. Never need he wear the despised uniform of the Habsburgs.

Joseph Conrad was taking tea in the garden of a country house outside Cracow in Austrian Poland when his hostess arrived with a telegram in her hand: 'General mobilization. Do you know? They are already taking the horses out of the ploughs and carts.'

'We had better go back to town as quickly as we can,' said Conrad.

As the Conrads passed through villages on the way, they saw mobs of horses on the commons with soldiers guarding them. Some old peasant women were already weeping aloud. When they arrived at their hotel the manager could scarcely be recognized. His hair, which had been luxuriant, was closely cropped. 'I shall sleep at the barracks tonight,' he explained.

'What are we to do, we Russian émigrés?' Leon Trotsky asked his friends among the Viennese Socialists. Old Friedrich Adler drove him to the headquarters of the political police. On the way Trotsky remarked, 'The war has given the country the appearance of being on holiday.'

'Those who rejoice,' Adler replied, 'are those who are not leaving for the front. Besides, you see all the unbalanced characters in the streets now. It is their moment. The murder of Jaurès is only a beginning.'

The Socialists thought sombrely over these words on the way to the police office. There Geyer, chief of the political police, told Trotsky that it was quite likely there would be an order next day for the internment of Russians and Serbs.

At ten past six that evening Trotsky and his family boarded the train for Zürich, leaving behind books, archives and unfinished work.

That night Joseph Conrad met some notabilities of Cracow.

For some reason or other, the electric light was not switched on, and the big room was lit only by a few tall candles, just enough for us to see each other's faces by. I saw in those faces the awful desolation of men whose country, torn in three, found itself engaged in the contest with no will of its own and not even the power to assert itself at the cost of life. . . . I remember one of those men addressing me after a period of mournful silence. . . . 'What do you think England will do?'

Conrad was not sure.

.   .   .   .   .

In Paris the streets were black with people, singing and carrying flags. German food shops were wrecked. Towards British visitors there was a notable coolness: '*Les Anglais, ils vont marcher, hein?*'

Britain was making up her mind, not without soul-searching. Soon after seven, Grey told the reassembled House that Belgium had rejected the German ultimatum. The debate continued. John Redmond, leader of the Irish Nationalists, declared, amid cheers, that the government could withdraw every one of its soldiers from Ireland. E. D. Morel said that if Germany threatened to annex Belgium or to occupy it, Britain would be bound to go to war. But she was being asked to fight because there might be a few German regiments in a corner of Belgian territory. In truth, she was going to war as much to preserve Russian despotism as to interfere with German ambition. The speaker was subjected to a continuous grumble of dissent.

Josiah Wedgwood warned the government that people were not the docile serfs they were a hundred years before. They could not put up with starvation. 'When it comes, you will see something far more important than a European war—you will see a revolution.' When Keir Hardie, another Labour spokesman, claimed that his was an international party which in France, Germany, Belgium and Austria was taking all manner of risks to preserve the peace, he was interrupted, 'Why don't they control the German emperor?' Hardie retorted, 'For the same reason that we don't control the Liberal Government, we aren't strong enough.' Arthur Ponsonby spoke sombrely: 'The war fever has begun. I saw it last night while I walked in the streets. Bands of half-drunken youths waving flags. A group outside a great club in St. James's Street being encouraged by members from the balcony. . . . The war fever has begun.'

The German Socialists met in Berlin to decide what they would do about voting war credits. By seventy-eight votes to fourteen, they decided to support the war. Haase, their leader, fell in with the views of the majority and agreed to read a statement of policy which, as a concession to Socialist philosophy, would denounce any war for annexation. This part of the statement was deleted that evening when it was submitted to Chancellor Bethmann Hollweg. The deletion was accepted without demur.

In the Russian Duma a Socialist deputy named Kerensky called on the workers and peasants to steel their spirit. 'When you have defended your country, liberate it!' Shustov, spokesman for the Bolshevist (Majority) Socialists, was even more defiant. 'We cannot prevent this war of emperors, but we will end it. This is the last act of barbarism!'

In his room Grey met Sir Arthur Nicolson, the implacable leader of the interventionists in the Foreign Office. The diplomat saw that his chief was at the end of his tether. He uttered a few words of congratulation on the speech. It had been a brilliant exposition, rendering a priceless service and transforming, at the eleventh hour, the whole atmosphere of the nation.

The Foreign Secretary, his face working, raised his fists high above his head and brought them crashing on the table.

'I hate war!' he cried. 'I hate war!'

Liverpool Street Station was in a state of turmoil, as holiday-makers, flocking back to London from the seaside resorts, jostled German reservists hurrying to the boat trains that would take them to Harwich and the beckoning Fatherland.

The British artist Charles Ricketts made up his diary for the day:

'Aug. 3. Occupation of Belgium definite, and under martial

law. This looks as bad as it can be. Walk through the Park. Exquisite light and cloud effects. By the time we reached Piccadilly, Sir Edward Grey's speech was on the placards and in the papers. As Shannon was reading it out to me in our little restaurant, cheering started down the street and a group of boys with flags passed. They stopped before our restaurant and booed the diners at the windows, who chanced to have long hair and looked like the new Cubist-post-Impressionist art students of today. . . . The little Italian waiter came up, a moment after; he said, sparkling with pleasure, 'The boss's brother left yesterday for Belgium, he is in the reserve force; he cried like a child on leaving his mother; I did not know a man could cry so much.'[1]

To Morley, evening came in his library, among his books, looking out on the trees and lawns of his house in Wimbledon Park. There John Burns brought him the news that Simon had recanted the resignation he had given that morning. A stroke of more exquisite irony was still to come. 'Beauchamp has been won over by the Prime Minister.' Remembering his conversation at luncheon, Morley could only smile. Earl Beauchamp would, after all, be the new Lord President of the Council! 'So you and I are the only two,' said Burns. Morley's eye fell, as it had often done before, on the quotation from Bacon carved deep in the granite of his mantelpiece: 'The nobler a soul is, the more objects of compassion it hath.'

1. *Self Portrait, Letters and Journals of Charles Ricketts*, ed. Cecil Lewis (Peter Davies, London).

16

Meeting of the Rifle Club Committee

Tuesday, 4 August

*F*OUR thousand three hundred trains, decorated with flowers and tricolour flags, and in some cases bearing chalked slogans like '*train de plaisir pour Berlin*',[1] overflowed with a noisy enthusiastic mass of young men in old-fashioned uniforms and resounded with an endless chanting of the 'Marseillaise'. The trains were carrying the French army towards the German army, which was moving to meet it in 11,000 trains.

The fighting spirit of the French soldiers was at a pitch unsurpassed since the revolutionary wars. Their equipment, apart from the field artillery, was not, however, equal to that of their enemy. Not enough heavy artillery, not nearly enough machine-

1. In a similar vein of humour, Austrian troop-trains were marked with 'Declarations of war to be left with the porter' (Nora Wydenbruck, *My Two Worlds*).

guns. As for uniforms, rarely have good soldiers gone to battle more unsuitably clad. They wore brilliant scarlet trousers and long, heavy greatcoats. On top of a pack weighing sixty pounds, each infantryman carried a faggot of dry wood with which to make a fire in his bivouac. Thus accoutred, he would march a hundred miles or more through some of the finest forests in Europe in the hottest August of the twentieth century.

Just promoted lieutenant, a very tall and awkward young Frenchman with a jutting nose marched from Arras towards the Belgian frontier with the 33rd Infantry Regiment, commanded by Colonel Pétain. His name was Charles de Gaulle. He did not yet suspect how ready staff officers are to believe anything that conforms with their plans or desires. It would no doubt have surprised him a great deal had he been told that the General Staff, after studying the mobilization plan of the German army, which had come into its possession, had decided that the plan was not genuine. For it showed that the Germans were launching eighty-eight divisions and fourteen Landwehr brigades against France whereas the French staff were sure that only sixty-eight German divisions would oppose them. Unfortunately the plan was right and the staff were wrong.

It was the second grave error of which the French Staff was guilty. The first had occurred ten years before when a letter signed '*Le Vengeur*' reached the French Chief of Staff. For 60,000 francs the writer would hand over the concentration plan which the Germans had worked out for a war against France. The offer was accepted. The insight obtained in this way was looked on with incredulity. In due course the *Vengeur* and his information were forgotten. And the French actually disarmed the main fortresses on their frontier with Belgium. For the contemptuous treatment given to the *Vengeur* document the excuse is made that, just then, French Intelligence was still disorganized by the Dreyfus Case. As for the *Vengeur* file, it was destroyed a few weeks after the opening of the great military operation which Count Schlieffen had designed.

. . . . .

While Lord Morley was nibbling his dry toast at breakfast in Wimbledon Park, a messenger from Downing Street brought a letter which Asquith had written at midnight the night before. It was an appeal. 'Think twice and thrice, and as many times more as arithmetic can number, before you take a step which impoverishes the government, and leaves me stranded and almost alone.' Morley paced the library, paced his garden, and then drove to his office in Whitehall. There he sat down and drafted his reply: 'Your letter shakes me terribly; it goes to my very core.' But 'to swear ourselves to France is to bind ourselves to Russia. . . . Again I say, divided counsels are fatal.'

The funeral procession of Jaurès moved slowly through brilliant sunlit streets from the Mairie of the 16th arrondissement to the Gare d'Orsay on the bank of the Seine. The red banners of the Socialists were draped with black. René Viviani, the Prime Minister, gave his arm to the widow. Léon Jouhaux, Secretary of the General Confederation of Labour, delivered the eulogy. Speaking as one who would leave to join his regiment next day, he declared, 'We take the field with the determination to drive back the aggressor.'

As Jouhaux spoke, so would the German Socialist leaders speak in a few hours' time.

A whole page of the *Manchester Guardian* was filled with an advertisement from the Neutrality League: '*Britons, Do Your Duty* and keep your country out of a wicked and stupid war.' The League[1] had not many days to live, and most of those who read

1. The League was formed 'a little before midnight on the Thursday before the August Bank Holiday' by Sir Norman Angell and some like-minded friends. 'Everybody was trooping out of town. So it meant hundreds of telegrams to people in the country and even abroad, in no mood to make the kind of decision which we were asking of them. We had managed to agree on the terms of a Manifesto.' Half a million leaflets were printed and distributed

and approved of its appeal were soon in soldiers' uniform. One of them was the writer of the newspaper's most powerful leading articles against the war, C. E. Montague. Aged forty-seven, he dyed his white hair an unconvincing yellow and persuaded a recruiting officer to let him enlist in the Sportsman's Battalion of the Royal Fusiliers.

The Times, at the head of its Personal Column, printed a small advertisement which expresses the romantic atmosphere of that bygone age and the hectic feeling of the moment: 'TO ALL WHO CALL THEMSELVES ENGLISH GENTLEMEN—are you DRILLED and ARMED and *ready* to DEFEND YOUR COUNTRY?' A few inches below, in the same column, the Austro-Hungarian government called on Landwehr and Honved men (i.e. reservists) in England to report without delay to the Consulate-General in London.

'There they are! Yes, there they are!' exclaimed the Belgian lieutenant, dropping his field glasses. From the wooded height where he and his men were standing, he had been able to make out the details of the grey uniforms of the lancers on the sunlit road to the east. Tearing a page from his pocket book, he wrote: 'Saw a Troop of uhlans in direction of Remouchamps, 4 August, 2 o'clock. Lieutenant Picard.'

'Pass me a pigeon.'

The troopers watched the bird for a moment as it flew off.

At three o'clock in the afternoon, in the hushed Chamber of Deputies, Paul Deschanel mounted the tribune. Everybody rose. The funeral oration of Jean Jaurès began . . . 'From the bier of this man rises a thought of union, from his icy lips a cry of hope. . . .' *Vive la France!* The deputies passed to other business, the speech

by 200 voluntary workers; 300 sandwich men patrolled the London streets. One enthusiast brought 500 sovereigns to Angell's chambers in the Temple. As the coins were poured over the table a prophet said: 'Take a good look! You will never see this sight again.'—Sir Norman Angell, *After All*.

of Viviani, a man at the end of his resources, a message from Poincaré. . . .

Beckoned by the ghost of Count Schlieffen, the grey flood of the German army poured into Belgium. At Verviers, obeying orders, they shouted '*Vive la Belgique!*' as they marched over the frontier line. The Belgians were not impressed by the friendly demonstration.

The Plan, on which Schlieffen had spent so many years, was the ultimate expression of the Prussian genius in degeneracy. The German army was a superb machine; the Schlieffen Plan was the working instructions that came with it. Both were delivered into the hands of Helmuth von Moltke the younger.

The strength of Prussia, and of the Germany it had created, lay in the military virtue of obedience. The simplest embodiment of that virtue was the private soldier on the parade ground obeying the drill sergeant: Left wheel!

The Schlieffen Plan was a drill sergeant's idea of strategy, a left wheel 200 miles across. 'Minds which have been trained mechanically triumph in peace-time over those possessing true insight and genius' (Scharnhorst). It involved breaking Germany's word and made it almost certain that Britain, bound in honour and interest to defend the neutrality of Belgium, would join the battle in the West at the side of France. But the more British soldiers on the Continent the better, said Moltke. The gendarmes would arrest them.

The British expeditionary force might be no more than 100,000 strong. But what kind of commander is he who scoffs at 100,000 men when they arrive on the battlefield on his side or the enemy's? And in addition to the British army, was there not the navy? The power of blockade?

In that critical summer there was a special reason for scepticism in Berlin and Paris too, about Britain's ability to wage war. The Irish feud had burned so deeply that many Europeans supposed that Ulster, which had landed German arms, would welcome a landing of German troops. The threat of civil war in Ireland, encouraged by fanatics, was a main factor in disturbing men's judgement. More than normally, the British army was discounted as a military instrument.

The Schlieffen Plan proves more conclusively than most examples in history how dangerous it is to allow the military virtues—that is to say, the vices of the parade ground—to dominate the instincts and imagination which can make out of glory, guesswork and logistics the clumsy art of war.

Moltke ordained and the ghost of Schlieffen led. The soldiers ordered, the ministers fell silent. 'It would have been too heavy a burden of responsibility,' said Bethmann Hollweg later, 'for a civil authority to have thwarted a military plan declared essential.' Thus the axiom of Bismarck's policy was made to stand on its head. And the German Chancellor donned his Dragoon Guards tunic to hear the Kaiser address the Reichstag.

The White Hall of the Old Palace in Berlin, where court balls were held, was a stately room with silvered mouldings, which had as an adornment of the centre of its parquet floor a crowned Prussian eagle. Here members of the Reichstag gathered, many of them in military uniform, to hear a speech from the throne. The Kaiser entered quickly and without fuss, accompanied by his military entourage and ladies of the imperial family. Bethmann, in his military uniform, towered over his master, who was only five foot six and looked small even with a spread-eagle helmet on his head. The Chancellor handed the Kaiser the text of the speech which Wilhelm then barked out in a loud staccato: 'We draw the sword with a clear conscience and with clean hands', etc., etc. He finished in strident tones, 'From this day on, I recognize no parties but only Germans!' The party leaders, deeply moved, sprang forward to clasp their Emperor's hand. The hall resounded with deep-throated *Hochs*!

Later, the Reichstag met again in its own building. Bethmann said that German troops were already in Belgium: 'Necessity knows no law . . . but what we are committing we will make good as soon as our military goal has been reached.' Thus, members of the Reichstag heard for the first time of a great moral catastrophe for Germany. Conservatives, Liberals and Socialists, they bore the news like men. But not everyone shared their equanimity. When Prince von Bülow read this portion of the Chancellor's speech in the newspaper he understood what children mean when they say, 'My heart stood still.'

A war credit of 5000,000,000 marks was voted unanimously by the Reichstag. Clemenceau's sardonic prediction was fulfilled: the Socialists were there, if not to the last man. Patriotism had found out the party which, seven days before, had declared, 'No German soldier's blood must be spilt to gratify the murderous intention of the Austrian tyrant.'

The Vienna Socialist newspaper *Arbeiteszeitung* was delighted with the vote: 'A day of the proudest and loftiest exaltation of the German spirit.' But the Russian political exile Lenin, living at Poronin in Austrian Poland, took a less enchanted view. When he read in *Vorwärts* the news of the Socialist vote in the Reichstag he exclaimed: 'Impossible! This copy is certainly a forgery by the German bourgeois canaille!' When at last the truth of the report was brought home to him, Lenin experienced one of his rare moments of despair. Even Leon Trotsky, watching events in Zürich and certainly possessing few illusions about the revolutionary fervour of the German Socialists, was surprised by the readiness with which they crawled on their stomachs before triumphant militarism. Another exile of the Russian revolutionary movement heard news of the war in Siberia, at Kureika on the lower reaches of the Yenisei River where a population of 10,000 Ostiaks and Russians were scattered over a territory about the size of Scotland. He was a Georgian, known in the movement as Stalin. Astute and ruthless, he shared the general Bolshevik view that the Tsar's war was the opportunity of the proletariat.

Sir Edward Grey received Mr. Walter Page, the American ambassador, at three o'clock: unless Germany called off her invasion of Belgium, Britain would declare war. He paused. 'Yet we must remember that there are two Germanys. There is the Germany of men like ourselves. Then there is the Germany of the war party. The war party has got the upper hand.' Sir Edward's eyes filled with tears. His voice shook. 'The efforts of a lifetime go for nothing.'

Page left the room, stunned by a sense of vast imminent ruin.

The House of Commons met at the usual hour and went through the usual preliminaries. But, as questions droned on, it was apparent that most members had their minds elsewhere. Colonel Burn asked about the prospect of an increase of pay for the civil staff at Darmouth Naval College. He was told that it was still under consideration. The Colonel made a half-hearted attempt to keep the controversy alive, looked round in protest and sat down. The moment had come.

The Prime Minister who had reached the House through crowds—described unkindly as composed of loafers and holiday-makers—spoke briefly and slowly, in a loud, hoarse voice. He said that Britain had sent an ultimatum to Germany asking for an assurance that the neutrality of Belgium would be respected. The ultimatum would expire at midnight. There were fervent and thoughtful cheers. All stood while he read a message from the King mobilizing the army.

Afterwards, in the quiet of his room, Asquith showed his wife Morley's letter. 'I shall miss him very much.'

'So it is all up?' asked Mrs. Asquith, whose mind was on a wider issue.

'Yes, it's all up.' They wept.

After that there was nothing to do but wait.

At 7 p.m. the British ambassador in Berlin, Sir Edward Goschen, handed to Bethmann an ultimatum, demanding that Germany should carry out her obligation to observe the neutrality of Belgium. Britain would wait until midnight (Central European time) for a reply. If Britain had betrayed a friend and broken her word, the hysterical indignation of the German Chancellor could not have been greater. Britain was 'stabbing a man from behind while he was fighting for his life'—and 'all for just a word, neutrality, just for a scrap of paper!'

Revealing and fatal, the phrase was duly reported to London by Goschen, who went back to his embassy to pack. 'One does not need to be a Machiavelli,' thought Bülow, 'to understand that if Bethmann really uttered this luckless expression, the supreme interests of the nation demanded that he should immediately and categorically deny it.' Too late! A good man, led through weakness of will and muddled thinking into a course of action which his conscience repudiated, Bethmann had in three words—and with a searing, suicidal vividness—set his own judgement on what he was doing. Through the rest of his life, the phrase haunted him, like the corpse of an albatross hung round his neck, reminding his fellow-countrymen that he, the student of Kant, the lover of Beethoven, had betrayed to a horrified world the unbridled and reckless impulses that were abroad in Germany.

From the slopes of the hill where they had halted, the Belgian scouts had a daunting spectacle under their eyes: A nightmare-like swarming of men, a prolonged clamour in which a thousand discordant sounds were confused. The immensity of the dusk was alive, and moving. Here and there, camp-fires reddened. They counted six cavalry regiments, two infantry regiments, one infantry battalion, one cyclist battalion and some artillery. Before them was the 9th German cavalry division.

The portrait of Sir Robert Walpole looked down from the wall of the Cabinet room on his successor. Once, on an outbreak of war, he had said, 'Now they ring the bells, but they will soon wring their hands.' Asquith and his wife, Grey and Lord Crewe sat in the gathering darkness until the clock on the mantelpiece struck eleven. No word had come from Berlin.

The last of the great European combatants stepped down into the arena. The iron circle of war was closed.

Pausing at the foot of the staircase on her way to bed, Mrs. Asquith caught sight of Winston Churchill, with a happy face, striding towards the double doors of the Cabinet room.

In the meantime the Foreign Office, to its horror, discovered that it had sent Prince Lichnowsky, along with his passport, a declaration of war which incorrectly assumed that the German Empire had declared war on Britain. Five minutes after the clock in the Cabinet room had ceased striking eleven, Harold Nicolson, a young clerk, took the Foreign Secretary's Rolls-Royce to drive to the German Embassy so that a correct version could be substituted. Lichnowsky pointed to a writing-table on which the envelope lay, half opened. Nicolson made the substitution and Lichnowsky signed a receipt. His Serene Highness collected his dignity and his manners.

'Give my best regards to your father,' he said.

After midnight a knock came to Norman Angell's door. It was Ramsay MacDonald, chairman of the Labour party. He threw himself on the sofa and, with his head in his hands, said: 'I have just resigned from the chairmanship. A man who has opposed our entrance into the war cannot lead a party that is going to support it.'[1]

In a Devon farmhouse, where he was staying, the English novelist John Galsworthy brooded over the horror of the thing in his diary entry for the day. 'If this war is not the death of Christianity, it will be odd. We need a creed that really applies humanism to life. . . . A meeting of the Rifle Club Committee.'

In the early hours of the morning, Henry James resumed writing a letter: 'The taper went out last night.'

1. Sir Norman Angell, *After All*, p. 189.

3

AFTERMATH

> *'This Europe, their Europe, which had become the mother and the teacher of all the countries of the earth, the source of all thought, of all invention, the guardian of all the secrets of mankind, was less precious to them now than was a flag, a national song, an accident of language, a frontier line, the name of a battle to be graven on a stone, a deposit of phosphate, the comparative statistics of ocean tonnage, or the pleasure of humiliating a neighbour.'*
> JULES ROMAINS, *'Men of Good Will'*

17

The Pride of Piccadilly

ON 5 AUGUST, or perhaps the day after, Prince von Bülow called on his successor, Theobald von Bethmann Hollweg, in the Wilhelmstrasse. Between these two Germans there was no bond of liking and not a great deal of respect. Bethmann found the Prince as smooth and treacherous as an icy pavement. He disliked Bülow's cynicism and resented his indefinable air of patronage. Bülow, for his part, believed Bethmann to be a bumbling amateur. And now, when amateurism had produced its grisly masterpiece, he could call on the victim, standing disconsolate amidst the ruins of his policy. There was an expression of compassionate concern on Bülow's plump, florid, handsome face that is reflected in the unconvincing pathos with which he describes the interview.

He was received in the drawing-room of the Chancellery. This apartment opens on to the garden with its splendid trees. A billiard room in Bismarck's time, it had been turned into an office where chancellors used to work in the heat of summer.

'Bethmann was standing in the middle of the room. I shall never forget his look, the expression of his eyes. . . . I asked, "Well tell me only how it happened?" He lifted his long arms to heaven and replied in a dead voice, "Ah, if only I knew!"'

'I have often regretted that no one took a snapshot of the Chancellor at the moment he said that to me; that photograph would be the best proof that the unhappy man had not wanted war.'

How, then, *did* it happen?

There are those who say that it could not have been avoided. But this fatalistic view is hardly borne out by a close inspection of the hurrying and, finally, headlong days in the capitals of Europe. At a dozen moments the road to a peaceful settlement was missed by no more than a hair's breadth.

Certainly vast changes were inevitable and not far off. Russia was going to plunge into a revolution of one kind or another. The Austro-Hungarian Empire could not survive unchanged in an age when nationalist enthusiasm was taking the place of dynastic loyalty as a cement of states. It was absurd to imagine that the Czechs could be denied their national claims or that the Hungarian nobility should for ever rule in Budapest. But there is no obvious reason why sweeping social and political changes must coincide with a general war.

Unless, indeed, Bethmann Hollweg was right when he cried out in despair that 'elemental forces' were unleashing a war that nobody wanted. An irrational ingredient was certainly present in the crisis and grew stronger as July burned into August and peace melted into war. Popular excitement flared into mass hysteria. Inflammatory songs were chanted. Flags fluttered in grey streets. The dangerous gaiety that Trotsky sensed in the Ring in Vienna spread to other capitals. And everywhere the final outcome was the same: Baron von Schoen was molested in his car in Paris; windows were broken at the British Embassy in Berlin, and at the

German Embassy in London. The Café Viennois in Paris was wrecked and looted. The police were called, always a little late. In St. Petersburg the patriotic mob went further: it stormed and pillaged Count Pourtalès's embassy. In that case, it was not certain which side the police were on. From the window of a club nearby, a general, waving a glass of champagne, encouraged the patriotic fury of the masses. The scene was faithfully reproduced elsewhere, by the well-dined orators outside Josty's Konditorei, and the zealots on the club balcony in St. James's Street.

But these disorders could hardly be called 'elemental forces'; they only reflected an intuition among idle people that their rulers could not handle the European crisis, that something was slipping out of control.

One truly elemental force was present throughout, steadily growing in strength and finally triumphant—Time. How often in the diplomatic documents of the period does the sad admission recur: 'Overtaken by events!' When Grey opened his apologies to the House he said that the pace had been forced. Forced it was, by the folly of a few men and the malice of some others, but also through the neglect of those who were neither fools nor criminals and who should have seen deeper and further into events and should have acted in time. There was no one with the stature, the imagination and the power to cry halt.

Jaurès might have done it, but only a Jaurès who could count on the European workers to follow him, or, failing that, had an armed nation at his back which he could launch or withhold as either action served the cause of peace.

Grey could have done it, but only a Grey who was ready to take real and terrible risks for peace—above all, the risk of tearing his own government apart, without any assurance of replacing it with a new government in alliance with the Conservatives. For it would have been necessary for him to speak sharply to French and Russians as well as to Germans and Austrians—to speak as the arbiter of Europe and not as a member of the Triple Entente. Above all, it would have been necessary to speak before the crisis had gathered too much momentum.

The decisive hours in the European crisis were, it seems, those that came crowding, one on the heels of another, after nine o'clock on the night of 29 July. During that time the balance after swinging for so long began to sink decisively towards war.

Grey sent a warning to Bethmann, and Bethmann, taking fright, passed it on to Berchtold. At that moment British and German diplomacy were at last acting in unison. Peace, as it seemed for a little while, was going to be saved. Austria, under German pressure, would agree to accept mediation after her troops had occupied Belgrade and appeased the sensitive honour of the Austrian army. Then suddenly the picture changed. Moltke broke in on the exchanges and urged Austria to mobilize against Russia. And Bethmann withdrew his appeal to Berchtold. The war was on!

Why this sudden reversal? It appears that the Kaiser had misunderstood a telegram from Nikky in St. Petersburg and had jumped to the erroneous conclusion that Russia had been mobilizing for four days. And, having preferred peace, through all the contradictions and absurdities of his policy, Wilhelm now suffered one of his emotional storms. He too must mobilize! And Moltke, who had his ears in the New Palace in Potsdam and learned of his volatile master's altered mood, seized the opportunity to intervene in Vienna.

Yet, as it turned out, this change of course in Berlin and Vienna was not the decisive factor it might have been. For while Berchtold oscillated between Bethmann's advice and Moltke's, the Tsar ordered a general mobilization of his army. From that moment, if the Russian autocrat did not rescind his ukase, the war was inevitable.

If Grey had spoken to Lichnowsky three days, even two days earlier, then events might have worked out differently. Bethmann might have applied the brake in Vienna without interference from his impulsive master. And Moltke would not have dared to intrude on the business of diplomacy.

It was, no doubt, necessary for Grey to go further than, in fact, he did. He must warn Russia through France as he warned Austria through Germany. He must frighten Viviani as he frightened Bethmann. He must convince Paris that—notwithstanding the Entente and the naval and military talks—British support for France in war would depend upon France imposing her brake on Russia's mobilization. The Tsar must not be allowed to mobilize unless Austria had rejected the 'Halt in Belgrade' and the idea of mediation.

This was certainly to ask a good deal of Grey: that he should see matters as plainly and steadily in the mad summer days of 1914 as they can be seen all these years later, and launch and carry out a resolute and independent policy which might not have the support either of his own party or of the opposition. It was perhaps to ask too much. But Grey was the key man in Europe vested with unique prestige and shining in moral authority. And his paramount duty was to save the peace.

In the summer of 1914 the forces of goodwill were far more impressive than those that worked for war. Who were the war-makers? Isvolski, Paléologue, Berchtold, Conrad, Moltke, Jagow. And perhaps Poincaré? Certainly the Lorrainer did not find war repugnant. On the other side were the Tsar, Tisza, the Kaiser, Bethmann Hollweg, Viviani, Grey. On the whole, the more impressive team, even if the Tsar was no mental giant and indolent, excitable Viviani was not a man of the calibre of Poincaré. But, as it turned out, the men of goodwill, for all their superiority in prestige and influence, were overcome, and the contrivers of anarchy triumphed. Paléologue blindfolded Viviani. Berchtold duped Tisza. Sukhomlinov deceived the Tsar. And, when the crunch came, there was Moltke standing ready with the match, and Poincaré at hand to blow on the flame!

But all these were essentially minor turns in the plot. They should never have been allowed to decide the issue. As Albert Ballin exclaimed in exasperation, 'One did not need to be a Bismarck to avoid *this* war!' But there was no Bismarck. Instead, there were:

The Kaiser, scribbling his stupid inflammatory marginal notes to dull the inward gnaw of caution which he mistook for timidity. A noisy, erratic, intellectually lazy man; the prisoner of his own romantic posturings. His power to disturb and frighten Europe should not be underrated among the factors that produced the crisis.

Bethmann Hollweg, a nobleman who was, by blood, half a banker, a bureaucrat who was half a philosopher, without the cunning or the authority of Bülow, above all, lacking in the tactical instinct which will guide a man through a tortuous and terrible crisis.

And Grey, by a perceptible margin the noblest of the cast.

He was a great English gentleman in the best and worst senses of the word. The soul of honour, he was incapable of shabbiness or conscious subtlety. He distrusted foreigners, combining this with a failure, either of will or ability, to communicate effectively with the mass of his own people. His impressive aloofness was another name for diffidence, and his diffidence masked a shrinking from disagreeable realities. One might say that in Grey's personality were to be found those elements in the English character which foreigners have found most admirable and most puzzling, above all, the knack of holding two contrary opinions simultaneously while remaining an honest man.

But Britain was a democracy. If her Foreign Secretary had no aptitude for leadership, if the triumvirate that ruled her foreign policy—Asquith, Grey and Haldane—had hugged the business of diplomacy to their bosoms like a sacred book, that could not be the end of the matter. There were other sources of guidance open to the public. There were the newspapers. What kind of instruction the Radical masses received in the crisis from their trusted prints has been seen. The leading articles in the *Manchester Guardian* and the *Nation* are remarkable for their energy and elegance—but how parochial in outlook, how selfish in spirit, how far below the level of events was the argument of those urgent and eloquent counsellors! 'We care as little for Belgrade as Belgrade does for Manchester.' And, above all, how remote from the realities of power in Europe! 'War, if it comes, will be due to the terms of the Entente with France', and to the military conversations that had gone secretly on since 1906. The influential leaderwriter said nothing of the danger that the German army might capture the ports of northern France and hand them over to the German navy, that Dunkirk and Cherbourg might become nests of German torpedo-boats and that the *Seydlitz* and *Derfflinger* battle-cruisers might find a base at Brest.

Contingencies like these had prompted the talks with the French staff officers and, by the summer of 1914, these contingencies had assumed a sinister air of immediacy.

The student of those days carries away the vivid impression that only in London and Berlin did the crisis bring to men any real anguish of mind. The Russians were fatalists, the Austrians gamblers, while the French were aware only that an enormous wrong was about to be righted. Forty-four years after the unjust verdict of Sedan, the Court of Appeal was about to sit. But the misery on Grey's face was matched by the misery on Bethmann Hollweg's.

The Chancellor was one of three men in Berlin who, from the beginning, were defeatists. The Kaiser and Tirpitz were the other two. Wilhelm knew in his heart that if the British came in they would never give up until they were beaten to their knees. The war would be long, and Germany needed a short war. As Tirpitz, the professional Britain-hater, saw it, Germany had been jockeyed into war six years before her fleet was ready. And he, of all men, was least likely to undervalue the strangling pressure of a British blockade. Bethmann Hollweg had counted throughout on victory for the non-interventionists in the Liberal Government. When, too late, he realized he had been wrong, he looked at the future with horror. As for Moltke, hastening to make war before it was too late to win, his was an optimism with a short term of life. If his army did not obtain a quick decision against the French, then Germany ought to make peace.

The situation in Berlin was, therefore, more complex than Grey believed it to be when he saw Germany as simply the supreme aggressor who, at all costs, must be baulked. Restless she was, aggressive and disturbing—but she was not a monolith. There were chinks in the masonry into which a diplomatic crowbar could have been driven.

Before the end of the year the illusions on which each of the great powers had gone to war lay in ruins. Austria had, at last, invaded Serbia, that 'nest of robbers and assassins', and had been driven ignominiously out again. Serbia was freed by 20 December. The Russians, who expected to be in Berlin by All Saints' Day, were annihilated at Tannenberg. The Germans, whose advance guard were due to enter the outskirts of Paris by the fortieth day, were checked at the Marne. The Schlieffen Plan, intricate masterpiece of Prussian staffwork, had failed. The French had planned to seize Lorraine in a glorious outburst of national élan. After assaults of fabulous courage and appalling cost the edge of the attack was blunted. By the end of the year, France had suffered casualties in battle as numerous as the total adult male population of the provinces she hoped to recover. As for the British, if they ever expected to destroy the German fleet in battle the delusion quickly evaporated. If they believed that they could fight the war with their imposing navy alone and that their small, admirable but ill-led expeditionary force was all they need send to the battlefields of Europe, that comfortable dream vanished with the autumn leaves. By the end of the year, Britain had a million soldiers under arms or, at least, in training. And very soon, her navy would be engaged in a desperate, unforeseen warfare with the German U-boats.

Moltke's staff said that the war would be over in six weeks. General Sir Henry Wilson, Director of Military Operations at the War Office, boasted, 'We should be in Elsenborn in four weeks.' And General Berthelot, assistant Chief of Staff to the French generalissimo, retorted, 'Three!' True, some considered that the ordeal might last longer. John Maynard Keynes, the Cambridge economist, thought that war might go on for a year or eighteen months. And Lord Kitchener was regarded as a man steeped in insensate gloom when he declared that the struggle would continue for three years or longer. On the whole, the armies expected to be home for Christmas.

When Christmas came and found them facing one another in miserable trenches, some British and some German soldiers fraternized, a brief intervention of good sense and human feeling which was sternly frowned on by higher authority. How much wiser if the politicians had joined in the Christmas truce instead of rebuking it!

By that time it was obvious the war would not be short and glorious but would be long, dreary and expensive. The only certainty about it was that, whoever might win, all would lose. And so it turned out.

Russia limped towards revolution. The Austro-Hungarian Empire, like a freighter whose cargo has shifted in worsening seas, broke up and sank. Britain's blockade squeezed the blood out of the German economy. France emerged as victor, in a graveyard:

> I saw a dead man win a fight
> And I think that man was I.

In 1921, after the reunion with Alsace-Lorraine, her population was smaller by 580,000 than it had been in 1914. She lost 1,315,000 men in battle. She made up the deficiency from other sources. In 1931, 2,700,000 aliens dwelt on French soil.

Britain, although less tragically, shared in the dismal triumph. Loaded with debts, she had neither the spirit nor the sinews to play any longer her old careless and arrogant role across the world.

One by one, the European empires moulted.

All this should have been already visible in outline to men of knowledge and imagination at the end of 1914. And by that time they could not put forward the excuse that they were at the mercy of mass hysteria. The popular clamour for the war was over. In truth, it did not long survive the glorious weather of that summer.

Thus the statesmen were no longer subject to the contagion of madness from the peoples.

They had, too, their own private visitations of remorse: 'To say I am oppressed by the thought of our responsibility for this war would be to say too little—The thought never leaves me. I live in it.' (Bethmann Hollweg.) 'It seems to me that, in the stillness of the night, I hear a voice which says, "You have betrayed your country".' (Janushkevitch.) To Berchtold conscience came wearing a different air. 'Leave me in peace,' said the Count one day in 1916, 'I was sick of the war long ago.'

But the war, which had insisted on coming to life, would not die simply because the fever of birth had subsided. It had a life of its own and bred its own race of leaders, resilient and fanatical, men who could be counted on to keep it alive after its original impetus had vanished. Asquith was followed by Lloyd George. Clemenceau in due course became Prime Minister of France. His policy was simple: '*Je fais la guerre.*' Ludendorff took over from Moltke and Falkenhayn. The nations, which had gone to war as if it were a public holiday, found themselves convicts in a chain gang and unable either to scheme or to fight their way to freedom. The generals were left with a war they did not know how to fight, the politicians with a peace they could not make. And the peoples? The *train de plaisir pour Berlin* stopped at Verdun, but the passengers were not permitted to alight. They were bound by pride and obstinacy to complete the journey. In their ears resounded unceasingly the call to suffer, to endure and to hate. Above all, to hate. The enemy, as the months passed, lost more and more of his semblance of humanity in official myth.

So Europe, which had begun to fight perhaps through a sheer excess of vitality, ended her war in exhaustion and ruin, too weary to fight any longer, too poisoned to make peace. Germany was punished, but not reconciled. France found the taste of revenge bitter in her mouth. Austria, the 'ramshackle empire', was destroyed—and replaced by arrangements still more ramshackle.

Russia withdrew into a fog of mystery, through which, from time to time, alarming new shapes of power could be discerned.

Europe's economic leadership among the continents disappeared. The United States assumed her role as the chief creditor, capitalist and banker of the world. She could well afford to take on this new responsibility: she would soon be *twice* as wealthy as the whole of Europe west of the Elbe. Nor could the outward flow of European population—and, therefore, culture and influence—be maintained at the old rhythm. The young men who might have colonized Africa, North and South, fell in Champagne and on the Somme. Apart from Russia, 6,000,000 European men were dead on the battlefields or in the hospitals.

With the surplus of physical energy something still more valuable had drained away from Europe: her moral authority. No doubt, it had been only a question of time before other continents seized economic leadership from her, but in making a spectacle of her own furious gift for self-destruction she lost her claim on the world's respect and on the deference of her own subjects. And this was a loss which she brought upon herself.

The financial, physical and spiritual decline of Europe took place over a generation, by stages, some of them spectacular, some of them painful. By the end of the process, the directorate which the continent had wielded over three-quarters of the globe had utterly vanished, to be replaced, after further agony, crime and madness, by a new system of power the main feature of which was a hegemony contested between the United States and Russia. By 1950, Europe had fallen so low that she could not defend herself unaided against Russia, once only a sleepy ogre sprawling between her and the East. Some of her most intelligent people even thought that never again would Europe be strong enough to man her own defences. In the summer of 1914 no thought would have appeared so paradoxical as that one.

Not only the vices and follies of the old Europe brought her down. Some of her more winsome qualities also turned against her.

The crochety Continent was not only the prophet and guide of civilization but also the custodian of certain precious particularities. When Jules Romains' hero tried to explain why Verdun still stood against the Germans in 1917 he spoke in turn of different types of Frenchmen, each of whom had a personal motive for fighting on. At last he came to the man who says simply: 'All that matters to me in this world is the language of France, the cathedrals of our French countryside, the quays of the Seine, landscapes that can be found nowhere else in the world, a way of life that is unique. If all that is to be taken away, life has no longer any point.'

Europe was filled with men, dumb or articulate, who felt thus about countries like France or England or Germany, about rivers like the Severn or the Seine, the Rhine, the Danube or the Volga. When they believed that a unique possession was suddenly in danger, they were, no doubt, unduly perturbed; the fabric of Europe is woven from threads that are tough as well as wonderful. But how noble and touching was the impulse to preserve it! Not only pride, not only folly, not only hatred and blood-thirstiness, but tenderness too played its part in the vast and deadly ferment. A tenderness akin to love.

The summer of 1914 wears a borrowed garland of pathos and loveliness. Looking back at it across a terrible gulf, those who remembered came to gild it with a special charm, a haunting beauty. The foliage of the trees in the Vienna woods was, as Stefan Zweig insisted afterwards, more lavish that year than in any season before. Osbert Sitwell wrote: 'The nights, sumptuous as they were, each with its own bloom of perfection on its surface, wore on.' In the great cities everywhere, a unique excitement reigned. Young people were granted more freedom than usual as if, with some premonition of what was to come, their elders were willing to loosen the reins of discipline.

On 5 August 1914 the pride of Piccadilly—and other streets— poured into the recruiting offices at Great Scotland Yard and elsewhere. They had come from watching Surrey play Notts at the Oval. They were sunburnt from a week-end at Brighton. They had been learning to dance the tango. On their lips were the tunes from the Alhambra or the Palace Theatre. Some of them carried away into grimmer scenes the memory of gorgeous settings of Le Coq d'Or or Petroushka, or of the scene outside Buckingham Palace last night when they had sung 'God Save the King' to the King.

But if the past had been full of colour and music, few of them supposed that the future would hold less excitement. Some of them had read in *The Times* that morning the advertisement seeking 'A patriotic, wealthy person to finance an ex-irregular officer to raise a regiment of mounted infantry'. The prospects were dangerous but romantic; the mood was confident. The young Guards officer who told his batman to pack his dress clothes for Christmas in conquered Germany thought in tune with the subaltern of the Gardes à Cheval in St. Petersburg who took his full dress uniform with him on the march in readiness for the triumphal entry of the Russian army into Berlin.

King George sent Sir Frederick Ponsonby to say farewell to Prince Lichnowsky while the Princess walked by the lake in St. James's Park weeping, and workmen unscrewed from the embassy door the brass plates with the imperial arms.

It was a beautiful summer morning, filled with a strange exhilaration which incautious young men waiting for the medical officer to listen to their hearts could easily mistake for a loosening of ancient shackles of every kind.

There was not a cloud in the sky.

Bibliography

A book which, like this one, concentrates its attention upon a few critical days in the life of Europe must necessarily use sources of different kinds and qualities. Upon Albertini's thorough study (*The Origins of the War of 1914*) of the intricate diplomatic pattern—to which tribute is paid elsewhere—I have drawn gratefully. For example, the suspicion that some reckless elements in St. Petersburg connived in the Sarajevo murder depends on his patient investigation. R. W. Seton-Watson's account in *Sarajevo* of the plot has been supplemented from Rebecca West's *Black Lamb and Grey Falcon* and other books.

Among diplomatic documents Karl Kautsky's collection (*Outbreak of the World War*), the despatches of Prince Lichnowsky (*Heading for the Abyss*) and the documents filched from the Imperial Russian Embassy in London and published by Siebert and Schreiner (*Entente Diplomacy and the World War*), have a particular interest as they deepen, or modify, Albertini's general picture.

Maurice Paléologue gives (in *An Ambassador's Memoirs*) a vivid picture of events in St. Petersburg. But Paléologue sometimes appears to be expanding and improving on contemporary notes: the conversations reported by this talented and eloquent witness do not always carry conviction. He is, however, an indispensable first-hand recorder of impressions in Russia, as Sir Edward Spears (*Liaison, 1914*) is in the case of Paris at the time of mobilization, Leon Trotsky (*My Life*) and Stefan Zweig (*The World of Yesterday*) are of popular emotions in Vienna.

Theodor Wolff's *The Eve of 1914* provides an expert, well-informed journalist's picture of Berlin at the time, its crowds, the part played by its leading political personalities, above all, the pathetic figure of Bethmann Hollweg. In a similar way, Jacques Chastenet's *Jours Inquiets et Jours Sanglants* has been drawn upon (along with authorities like D. W. Brogan—*The Development of Modern France*—and Messimy's *Mes Souvenirs*) to give background to the account of the Caillaux Trial. Caillaux's own *Memoirs* must be read with caution on account

217

of his political animosities. For the trial itself, newspaper reports, English and French, have been drawn upon.

The desperate efforts of Jean Jaurès to stave off war, his murder and its aftermath—for these Marcelle Auclair (*La Vie de Jean Jaurès*), Hampden Jackson (*Jean Jaurès*), Emil Ludwig (*July 1914*) and contemporary newspapers have been used.

The British crisis has been seen as largely a struggle of conscience within the Liberal Cabinet, party and public. To Lord Morley's illuminating account of events in the Cabinet, the testimonies of Asquith, Grey, Churchill, Haldane, Samuel, Simon and others have been added. The Liberal newspaper comment of the time, notably that in the *Manchester Guardian*, has been examined to establish the strength of the current of argument against the war.

Several sources have been read in search of valuable and graphic sidelights—Pearl Adam's *Paris Sees It Through*, Constantine Benckendorff's *Half a Life*, H. Galli's *La Guerre à Paris*, David Garnett's *The Golden Echo* (especially for an anecdote about J. M. Keynes), John Galsworthy's *Diary*, the *Letters* of Henry James, Arthur Koestler's *Arrow in the Blue*, Michael Macdonagh's *In London During the Great War*, Pound and Harmsworth's *Northcliffe* (especially for the light it throws on policy-making in *The Times* office) and John Evelyn Wrench's *Struggle, 1914-1920*, valuable reminiscences by a journalist who was sent to Paris by Northcliffe a day or two before war broke out.

Over and over again I have found fresh light upon those extraordinary days in the columns of the newspapers. They provide something which, for my purpose, was as valuable as the pondered judgements of the historian—the rough and immediate jottings of men under whose gaze history was being made and catastrophe was being brought nearer at lightning speed.

This bibliographical note contains only a small portion of the sources I have consulted. A completer list is appended.

Adam, H. Pearl: *Paris Sees It Through*, Hodder & Stoughton (London, 1919).

Addison, Christopher: *Politics from Within*, Herbert Jenkins Ltd. (London, 1924).

Albertini, Luigi: *The Origins of the War of 1914* (3 vols), Oxford University Press (1924-43).

Angell, Norman: *The Great Illusion*, William Heinemann Ltd. (London, 1910).

Arthur, Sir George: *Life of Lord Kitchener*, Macmillan & Co. (London, 1920).

Asquith, Earl of Oxford &: *Memories and Reflections*, Cassell & Co. Ltd. (London, 1928).

Asquith, Margot: *Autobiography, Vol. II*, Thornton Butterworth Ltd. (London, 1920–22).

Auclair, Marcelle: *La Vie de Jean Jaurès*, Editions du Seuil (Paris, 1954).

Barrès, Maurice: *L'Union Sacrée*, Librairie Plon (Paris, 1915–19).

Beaverbrook, Lord: *Politicians and the War*, Thornton Butterworth Ltd. (London, 1928–32). Later published in one volume by Oldbourne Press.

Benckendorff, Constantine: *Half a Life: The Reminiscences of a Russian Gentleman*, The Richards Press (London, 1954).

Bertie, Lord: *Diary*, Hodder & Stoughton Ltd. (London, 1924).

Bethmann Hollweg, Theobald von: *Reflections on the World War*, Thornton Butterworth Ltd. (London, 1920).

Blond, Georges: *La Marne*, Presses de la Cité (Paris, 1963).

Brogan, D. W.: *The Development of Modern France*, Cassell & Co. Ltd. (London, 1940).

Buchanan, Sir George: *My Mission to Russia*, Cassell & Co. Ltd. (London, 1923).

Bülow, Prince Bernard von: *Memoirs* (4 vols.), Putnam (London and New York, 1931–32).

Caillaux, Joseph: *Mes Mémoires*, Librairie Plon (Paris, 1942–47).

Callwell, Sir Charles E.: *F. M. Sir Henry Wilson*, Cassell & Co. Ltd. (London, 1927).

Chamberlain, Sir Austen: *Down the Years*, Cassell & Co. Ltd. (London, 1935).

Chamberlain, Sir Austen: *Politics from Inside*, Cassell & Co. Ltd. (London, 1936).

Chastenet, Jacques: *Jours Inquiets et Jours Sanglants*, Librairie Hachette (Paris, 1952–62).

Churchill, W. S.: *The World Crisis*. Vol. I, Thornton Butterworth Ltd. (London, 1923).

Conrad von Hötzendorf, Count Franz: *Aus Meiner Dienstzeit*, Rikola Verlag (Vienna, 1921–25).

Conrad, Joseph: *Notes on Life and Letters*, Dent (London, 1921).

Bibliography

Czernin, Graf von: *In the World War*, Cassell & Co. Ltd. (London, 1919).
Deville, Robert: *Carnet de route d'un artilleur*, Chapelot (Virton la Marne, 1916).
Dumaine, Jacques: *La Dernière Ambassade*, Librairie Plon (Paris, 1921).
Fay, S. B.: *Origins of the War*, The Macmillan Co. (New York, 1929).
Fisher, M. and J.: *Shackleton*, Barrie (London, 1957).
Fitzroy, Sir Almeric: *Memoirs*, Hutchinson (London, 1925).
Florinsky, Michael T.: *The End of the Russian Empire*, Yale University Press (New Haven, 1931).
Fyfe, Hamilton: *The Making of an Optimist*, Leonard Parsons (London, 1921).
Galli, H.: *La Guerre à Paris*, Librairie Garnier Frères (Paris, 1917).
Galsworthy, John: *Diary* (see *The Life and Letters of John Galsworthy* by H. V. Marrot), Heinemann (London, 1935).
Gardiner, A. G.: *Prophets, Priests and Kings*, Alston Rivers (London, 1917).
Garnett, David: *The Golden Echo*, Chatto and Windus (London, 1953).
Gerard, James W.: *My Four Years in Germany*, Hodder & Stoughton Ltd. (London, 1917).
Gooch, G. P.: *Before the War*, Longmans Green (London, 1936–38).
Gourko, Vladimir: *Features and Figures of the Past*, Stanford University Press (1939).
Grasset, A.: *Vingt jours de Guerre Aux Temps Héroiques*, Berger-Levrault (Paris, 1919).
Grey, Lord, of Falloden: *Twenty Five Years* (3 vols), Hodder & Stoughton Ltd. (London, 1925).
Guyot, Yves: *Les Causes et les Conséquences de la Guerre*, Felix Alcan (Paris, 1915).
Haldane, Lord: *An Autobiography*, Hodder & Stoughton Ltd. (London, 1919).
Haldane, Lord: *Before the War*, Cassell & Co. Ltd. (London, 1920).
Halevy, Elie: *The World Crisis, 1914–18*, Oxford University Press (1930).
Hamilton, Lord Frederick: *Vanished Pomps of Yesteryear*, Hodder & Stoughton Ltd. (London, 1919).
Hammond, J. L.: *C. P. Scott*, Bell (London, 1934).
Hantsch, Hugo: *Leopold, Graf Berchtold*, Verlag Styria (Wien, 1963).
Harrod, R. J.: *The Life of John Maynard Keynes*, Macmillan (London, 1951).

Hendrick, Burton J.: *Life and Letters of Walter H. Page*, Vol. I, William Heinemann Ltd. (London, 1922–25).

Hitler, Adolf: *Mein Kampf* (trans. *My Struggle*), Hurst & Blackett (London, 1939).

Huldermann, Bernhard: *Albert Ballin*, Cassell & Co. (London, 1922).

Jackson, Hampden: *Jean Jaurès*, Allen & Unwin (London, 1934).

James, Henry: *The Letters*, Vol. 2, Macmillan & Co. (London, 1920).

Kautsky, Karl: *Outbreak of the World War: German documents*, Oxford University Press (1924).

Knox, Sir Alfred: *With the Russian Army*, Hutchinson & Co. (London, 1921).

Koestler, Arthur: *Arrow in the Blue: an autobiography*, Hamish Hamilton (London, 1952).

Kurenberg, Joachim von: *The Kaiser*, Cassell & Co. (London, 1954).

Lanyi, Ladislas: *Le Comte Etienne Tisza*, Lagny (Paris, 1946).

Lichnowsky, Prince Karl: *Heading for the Abyss*, Constable & Co. (London, 1928).

Lloyd George, David: *War Memoirs*, Ivor Nicholson & Watson (London, 1933–36).

Lombard, Laurent: *Ceux de Liège*, G. Lens (Verviers, 1934).

Ludwig, Emil: *July 1914*, G. P. Putnam & Sons Ltd. (London and New York, 1929).

Ludwig, Emil: *Wilhelm II*, G. P. Putnam & Sons Ltd. (London and New York, 1926).

Lutz, Herrmann: *Grey and the World War*, George Allen & Unwin Ltd. (London, 1928).

Macdonagh, Michael: *In London During the Great War*, Eyre & Spottiswoode (London, 1935).

Mackworth, Cecily: *Guillaume Apollinaire*, John Murray (London, 1961).

Mansergh, Nicholas: *The Coming of the First World War*, Longmans, Green & Co. (London, 1949).

Margutti, Albert von: *La Tragédie des Hapsbourgs*, G. Cres (Paris, 1924).

Martin, William: *Statesmen of the War*, Jarrold (London, 1928).

Maurice, Frederick: *Haldane: The Life of Viscount Haldane of Cloan*, Faber & Faber (London, 1937–39).

Messimy, Adolphe: *Mes Souvenirs*, Librairie Plon (Paris, 1937).

Moltke, Helmuth von: *Erinnerungen etc.*, Der Kommende Tag (Stuttgart, 1922).

Bibliography

Morel, E. D.: *Truth and the War*, National Labour Press (Manchester, 1916).

Morgan, John H.: *John, Viscount Morley*, John Murray (London, 1924).

Morley, Lord: *Memorandum on Resignation*, Macmillan & Co. (London, 1928).

Müller, Georg von: *The Kaiser and his Court*, Macdonald (London, 1961).

Musulin, Freiherr Alexander von: *Das Haus am Ballplatz*, Verlag für Kulturpolitik (Munich, 1924).

Nicolson, Harold: *Sir Arthur Nicolson, Bart., First Lord Carnock*, Constable & Co (London, 1930).

Nicolson, Harold: *King George the Fifth*, Constable & Co. (London, 1952).

Paléologue, Maurice: *An Ambassador's Memoirs*, Librairie Plon (Paris, 1923–25).

Paléologue, Maurice: *Journal 1913–14*, Librairie Plon (Paris, 1947).

Poincaré, Raymond: *Memoirs 1913–14*, William Heinemann Ltd. (London, 1926–30).

Pound, Reginald and Harmsworth, Geoffrey: *Northcliffe*, Cassell & Co. (London, 1959).

Radziwill, Princess Catherine: *The Austrian Court from Within*, Cassell & Co. (London, 1916).

Recouly, Raymond: *Les Heures Tragiques D'Avant Guerre*, La Renaissance du Livre (Paris, 1922).

Renouvin, Pierre: *La Crise Européene et la Première Guerre Mondiale*, Presses Universitaires de France (Paris, 1934).

Rumbold, Sir Horace: *The War Crisis in Berlin*, Constable (London, 1940).

Samuel, Viscount: *Memoirs*, The Cresset Press (London, 1945).

Sazonov, Sergei: *Fateful Years. Reminiscences*, Jonathan Cape (London, 1928).

Schmitt, Bernadotte E.: *The Coming of the War*, Charles Scribners' Sons (New York, London, 1930).

Seton-Watson, R. W.: *Sarajevo*, Hutchinson & Co. (London, 1926).

Siebert, B. von and G. A. Schreiner: *Entente Diplomacy and the World War*, Geo. Allen & Unwin (London, 1923).

Simon, Sir John: *Retrospect*, Hutchinson & Co. (London, 1952).

Sitwell, Sir Osbert: *Great Morning*, Macmillan (London, 1945–50).

Spears, Edward: *Liaison, 1914*, William Heinemann Ltd. (London, 1930).

Spender, J. A. and Asquith, Cyril: *Life of H. H. Asquith*, Hutchinson & Co. (London, 1932).

Spender, J. A.: *Fifty Years of Europe*, Cassell & Co. (London, 1933).

Steed, H. Wickham: *Doom of the Hapsburgs*, Arrowsmith (1914).

Stein, General von: *A War Minister and his Work*, Skeffington (London, 1920).

Szilassy, Baron J. von: *Der Untergang der Donau-Monarchie*, Verlag Neues Vaterland (Berlin, 1921).

Thibaudet, Albert: *Les Princes Lorrains*, Grasset (Paris, 1924).

Thoumin, Richard: *La Grande Guerre*, Julliard (Paris, 1962) (Published in England as *The Great War*, Secker & Warburg, 1963).

Tirpitz, Alfred von: *My Memoirs*, Hurst & Blackett Ltd. (London, 1919).

Topham, Anne: *Memories of the Kaiser's Court*, Methuen (London, 1914).

Trevelyan, G. M.: *Grey of Falloden*, Longmans, Green & Co. (London, 1937).

Trotsky, Leon: *My Life*, Thornton Butterworth Ltd. (London, 1930).

Tuchman, Barbara W.: *The Guns of August*, The Macmillan Co. (New York, 1962).

West, Rebecca: *Black Lamb and Grey Falcon*, Macmillan & Co. (London, 1942).

Wolff, Theodor: *The Eve of 1914*, Victor Gollancz (London, 1935).

Wrench, John Evelyn: *Struggle 1914–1920*, Ivor Nicholson and Watson (London, 1935).

Zedlitz-Trutschler, R. V.: *Twelve Years at the German Court*, Nisbet & Co. (London, 1924).

Zweig, Stefan: *The World of Yesterday*, Cassell & Co. (London, 1943).

Also the files of *The Times, Daily Express, Daily News, Morning Post, Manchester Guardian, Figaro, Matin, Illustrated London News, Illustration, Nation, New Statesman, The Times Literary Supplement* (11 December 1948), *Le Monde* (12 February 1958), *Hansard*.

Index

Index

Index